THE
GREAT
TENOR TRAGEDY

THE LAST DAYS OF
ADOLPHE NOURRIT
AS TOLD (MOSTLY) BY HIMSELF

———————

Edited, Annotated, and with an Introduction
and Epilogue by Henry Pleasants

Translations by Henry and Richard R. Pleasants

AMADEUS PRESS
Reinhard G. Pauly, General Editor
Portland, Oregon

Credits for illustrations and text appear on page 181.

Copyright © 1995 by Amadeus Press
(an imprint of Timber Press, Inc.)
All rights reserved.

ISBN 0-931340-89-6

Printed in Singapore

AMADEUS PRESS
The Haseltine Building
133 S.W. Second Avenue, Suite 450
Portland, Oregon 97204, U.S.A.

Library of Congress Cataloging-in-Publication Data

Nourrit, Adolphe, 1802–1839.
    The great tenor tragedy : the last days of Adolphe Nourrit / as
told (mostly) by himself; edited, annotated, and with an
introduction and epilogue by Henry Pleasants; translations by
Henry and Richard R. Pleasants.
        p.   cm.
    Includes index.
    ISBN 0-931340-89-6
    1. Nourrit, Adolphe, 1802–1839—Last years. 2. Nourrit,
Adolphe, 1802–1839—Death and burial. 3. Tenors (Singers)—
France—Biography. I. Pleasants, Henry. II. Title.
ML420.N785A3 1995
782.1'092—dc20
[B]   94-49112
                                                         CIP
                                                         MN

CONTENTS

Preface vii

Introduction 1

Part 1   FRANCE: Withdrawal from the
Opéra and Provincial Tour . . 9

Part 2   ITALY: Turin, Genoa, Milan, Venice,
Florence, Rome, Naples . . . 29

Part 3   ITALY: The Student (Donizetti
and the Preparation of *Poliuto*) . 43

Part 4   ITALY: The Artist (Success, Failure,
Success, Disappointment, Despair,
Disaster) 83

Epilogue   Riddle Me This 125

Postscripts   Diagnosis in Retrospect • Nourrit
as Others Saw and Heard Him •
The Three Tenors of the 1830s . 133

Notes   163

Index   175

Plates follow page 82

PREFACE

The career, initially glorious, then distressing, finally tragic, is familiar, if only in bold outline, to most students of opera history. Unfamiliar are the intimate details of the personal and artistic Odyssey that ended in suicide. It is with these that we shall be concerned.

Adolphe Nourrit (1802–1839) was the greatest singing actor of his time. He sang at the Paris Opéra (Académie Royale de Musique) from 1821 to 1837, succeeding his father, Louis Nourrit (1780–1831), as principal tenor in 1824. His achievements during his thirteen-year reign were unprecedented, and remain unequaled.

No other tenor has created so many important roles: Néoclès in Rossini's *Le siège de Corinthe* (1826); Aménophis in Rossini's *Moïse* (1827); Masaniello in Auber's *La muette de Portici* (1828); Count Ory in Rossini's *Le Comte Ory* (1828); Arnold in Rossini's *William Tell* (1829); Robert in Meyerbeer's *Robert le diable* (1831); Gustave in Auber's *Gustave III* (1833); Éléazar in Halévy's *La Juive* (1835); and Raoul in Meyerbeer's *Les Huguenots* (1836).

He withdrew from the Opéra after his triumph as Raoul

rather than share leading roles with Gilbert-Louis Duprez (1806–1896),[1] newly returned to Paris after a brilliant career in Italy, which was crowned by the creation of the role of Edgardo in Donizetti's *Lucia* in Naples in 1835. When a tour of the French provinces, following an emotional farewell at the Opéra on 1 April 1837, was cut short by illness and a vocal and mental collapse in Marseilles, Nourrit journeyed to Italy, prompted by Duprez's example, to learn to sing in the new Italian style and to seek a new career as a singer of Italian opera.

He studied with Donizetti in Naples, and sang there, not without success, most notably in the Neapolitan premiere of Mercadante's *Il giuramento*. Donizetti even composed an opera for his Italian debut, *Poliuto*, set to a scenario by Nourrit that drew upon Corneille's *Polyeucte*. It was forbidden on religious grounds by the Neapolitan censorship.

Unable or unwilling to accept or adapt himself to what he soon discovered to be the exigencies, requirements, conventions, and repertoire of the Italian opera houses, and plagued by vocal problems and failing health, he fell into a state of depression, melancholia, paranoia, and despair, and ended by throwing himself to his death from the top floor of his Neapolitan residence early in the morning of 8 March 1839, just four days after his thirty-seventh birthday.

He was not just a singer. As a man of the theater he was more singing actor than acting singer, and his advice and collaboration were sought by composers in matters of dramatic structure and text. As a poet he wrote the words to Éléazar's "Rachel, quand du Seigneur" in *La Juive*, and he

collaborated in the translation of some of Schubert's songs
which he introduced to France (and to which he had been
introduced by Liszt, with whom he often sang them). He
wrote the scenarios to four ballets. In 1827, still only twenty-
five, he was appointed to a professorship *de déclamation* at
the Conservatoire.

But these facts tell us nothing of the personal drama and
trauma that lay behind them in the last two years. The details
of Nourrit's life and career are exhaustively and fastidiously
documented in Louis Quicherat's *Adolphe Nourrit: Sa Vie,
Son Talent, Son Caractère, Sa Correspondance* (Paris, 1867).
Quicherat was Nourrit's schoolmate at Sainte-Barbe and remained an intimate friend of the tenor and his family. The
biography is in three volumes, the third devoted to the correspondence. It is this third volume, and specifically its un-
folding of the tragedy, largely as related by Nourrit himself,
that shall concern us in the following pages.[2]

I read some of this correspondence more than thirty years
ago while preparing the chapter on Nourrit for my book *The
Great Singers: From the Dawn of Opera to Our Own Time*.[3] I
was so moved by the content and character of Nourrit's letters to his wife that I asked my brother, Richard, a retired in-
structor in French at the Groton School in Groton, Massachusetts, to translate them for me, having in mind no more
than a possible article or memoir. My brother obliged.

As I was then engaged with my translation of the music
criticisms of Hugo Wolf[4] and subsequently with the translation of the collected writings of Friedrich Wieck (Clara Schumann's father and teacher),[5] I put his work aside for future

reference. When the way was finally clear for me to return to Nourrit, my brother had died (March 1987).

Reviewing what he had done, I found myself referring back to the original correspondence, and in so doing became more and more absorbed in what I had *not* asked my brother to translate: the tenor's correspondence with others after his wife had joined him in Naples in June of 1838 and also correspondence from others relative to those last months. It became apparent to me that the substance and detail of this correspondence went far beyond what could be summarized adequately in an article: an appalling personal tragedy played out against a fascinating background of opera history in France and Italy in the 1830s—in other words, before the emergence of Verdi and Wagner.

I had to choose between seeking a new translator—in which case I would have had to supervise the selection of letters, do the editing, and add the annotation—and undertaking the translation myself. Although I had not previously translated from French for publication, I chose the latter course. Thus, the translation of Nourrit's letters to his wife is my brother's, here gratefully acknowledged. All else is mine, and I assume responsibility for it.

In selecting from this voluminous correspondence, and from the individual letters, my objective has been to sustain the narrative, omitting salutations, valedictories, discussion of irrelevant family matters, accounts of sight-seeing, weather reports, and other incidental remarks, as well as undue repetition.

I close this preface by observing that never before have I dealt with a subject in which I found myself becoming so emotionally involved. I hope that my readers may share this identification with one of the most searing personal tragedies of opera history, its victim one of the greatest, most gifted, most accomplished, most sympathetic, and certainly one of the most dedicated of its many great artists.

THE GREAT TENOR TRAGEDY

INTRODUCTION

It is a commonplace of opera talk nowadays to speak of "the three tenors"—José Carreras, Plácido Domingo, and Luciano Pavarotti. Not far behind them in celebrity in recent years have been such tenors as Carlo Bergonzi, Franco Corelli, Giuseppe di Stefano, Nicolai Gedda, and Richard Tucker. Earlier in the century we have had Jussi Bjoerling, Enrico Caruso, Beniamino Gigli, Tito Schipa, Giacomo Lauri-Volpi, Max Lorenz, Giovanni Martinelli, Lauritz Melchior, Aureliano Pertile, Helge Roswaenge, and Richard Tauber.

It must come, then, as something of a surprise to the lay opera-lover and tenor enthusiast to be told that for the first two of opera history's four centuries, the tenor did not count for much. He was there, but rarely in a starring role. He played second fiddle to others of his gender, but they were not tenors.

They were sopranos—or altos—castrated before puberty to preserve and enlarge upon a boyish treble. Their dominion—and the surgical practice, or practices, associated with it—ended with the social enlightenment following the French Revolution around the dawn and into the early years

1

of the nineteenth century. They were succeeded in *opera seria* and other serious opera, such as the French *tragédie-lyrique*, by female contraltos and mezzo-sopranos—and tenors. The female soprano had always been there except in regions where the appearance of females in the theater (as well as audibly in church) was forbidden.

It is tempting to think of Adolphe Nourrit as the first of these tenors to whom the adjective *great* can be applied. Certainly he was *great*, but he was not the first. That distinction rests beyond question with the Italian Giovanni-Battista Rubini (1794–1854), eight years Nourrit's senior, who was Bellini's tenor (*I Puritani* and *Il pirata*) just as his forerunners, Andrea Nozzari (1775–1832), Giovanni David (1790–1864) and Manuel García (1775–1832) had been the tenors of Rossini's earlier Italian operas.

But there was an important distinction. Rubini, as a singer, in his vocal production and interpretive style reflected the older art of the castrati, with much virtuoso and ornamental employment of mixed voice, head voice, and falsetto. He was always more singer than actor, if, indeed, he could be thought of as an actor at all. Nourrit, if not more actor than singer, was ever at pains to make his singing a projection and extension of the actor's art, and he was as attentive to matters of deportment, gesture, makeup, facial expression, and costume as he was to vocalism.

In that sense, he was indeed the first as creator of a new genre of dramatic tenor in roles fashioned for him, often with his collaboration with respect to text, continuity, contrast, costume, and decor, by Rossini, Auber, Halévy, and, above all, Meyerbeer. The latter, when referring to *Les Huguenots* in his letters to Nourrit, always spoke of "our opera, which owes more to you than to the author."[1]

The two singers were contemporaries in Paris in the 1820s and 1830s, Rubini at the Théâtre-Italien, Nourrit at the Opéra. They knew each other and were on friendly, if not intimate, terms, each recognizing the other's worth. Quicherat describes the relationship succinctly:

> The two artists entertained much esteem and affection for one another. One day Nourrit was holding forth in praise of Rubini to a small group of friends. One of them said: "Just recently Rubini was speaking in the same terms of you!" Each of the two secretly acknowledged to the other his own shortcomings. Perfection would have been found in a merger of their respective attributes.[2]

If Nourrit was, then, the first great *dramatic* tenor, indeed, the creator of the category, his eminence was also essentially transitional, as was the repertoire in which he dominated the Paris opera scene for thirteen years. He lacked the full-voiced upper register that his successors, beginning with Duprez, brought to the roles he had created and to roles written for them by Meyerbeer (*Le prophète* and *L'Africaine*) and later composers, most notably Verdi.

The writing had appeared on the wall in the early 1820s when Rubini's older contemporary, Domenico Donzelli (1790–1873), Rossini's first Otello and Bellini's first Pollione (*Norma*), astounded his listeners with a full-voiced high A.

Donzelli is credited as the initiator of the tenor *voix sombrée* (darkened voice) that brought greater weight and dramatic vehemence, not to mention athletic excitement, to vocal utterance—and shortened the careers of many of those who employed it, including Donzelli and, in due course, Duprez, who took it up another minor third to the full-voiced high C (*ut de poitrine*), or C from the chest. It was Nourrit's reading of that writing on the wall that prompted his ultimate journey to Italy, following the example of Duprez.

It may take a moment's reflection to accept Nourrit's repertoire as transitional. Some of the operas and roles written for him—*Robert le diable*, *William Tell*, Éléazar in *La Juive*, and Raoul in *Les Huguenots*—endured in the repertoire in Paris and elsewhere for close to a century. Though they are now seldom encountered in the opera house, due primarily to their inordinate length, the cost of staging, and the difficulty of casting them, their music is easily available and accessible on record.

And yet in retrospect they do represent a transition—however extended—from opera as it was prior to around 1820 to opera as it is familiar to us in the theater today in the works of Verdi, Wagner, Strauss, Mascagni, Leoncavallo, Giordano, Gounod, Massenet, and Bizet, among others.

Quicherat, in volume one of his Nourrit biography, gives a lucid account of the opera world of Paris as it was in 1821 when Nourrit arrived on the scene, an essential factor being the impending drift of Europe's operatic center from Italy to France.

The Opéra at that time—here I am drawing upon Quicherat, but not exclusively—in contrast to the livelier, more adventurous, more popular and prosperous Opéra-Comique and to the vocal splendors and Italian repertoire of the Théâtre-Italien, languished in the hands and minds of a traditionalist establishment still wedded to the concept of serious opera as *tragédie-lyrique*, with French declamation valued above Italianate lyricism, a holdover from the famous contention between the Gluckists and the Piccinnists of half a century earlier (1777–81).

Nourrit, significantly, made his debut at the Opéra, when he was not yet twenty, as Pylades in Gluck's *Iphigénie en Tauride* (10 September 1821). In his early seasons at the Opéra he also appeared as Renaud in Gluck's *Armide* and took over his father's tenor role of Orphée in Gluck's French revision of *Orfeo ed Euridice*.

"If the Opéra," writes Quicherat, "had continued as it was, that is to say in the same rut, Adolphe Nourrit would have had an obscure career. The examples he had before his eyes, and his native modesty, would not have prompted him to dream of any other success. A man of genius was to change the face of things and steer the art into a broader channel. Rossini was the catalyst."[3]

Rossini first came to Paris in 1823, already a celebrity. Twelve of his operas had been produced with great success at the Théâtre-Italien, then under the direction of Ferdinando Paër. Among its artists was Manuel García, Rossini's first Almaviva in *Il barbiere di Siviglia*, who also sang in its Paris premiere. More important to our subject, García had also been the vocal teacher of Adolphe Nourrit.

Rossini was only a transient during that first visit, but he returned in 1825 to share with Paër (briefly) the directorship of the Théâtre-Italien and to prepare a new work for the Opéra. This would be *Le siège de Corinthe*, a complete refashioning in French of his earlier *Maometto II* (1820). The Paris premiere was on 9 October 1826, with Nourrit in the principal tenor role of Néoclès. It was a stunning and enduring success.

But as codirector of the Théâtre-Italien, Rossini contributed more than a work of his own to the changing face of opera in Paris—and to the future career of Nourrit. He brought in from Italy the German Giacomo Meyerbeer (born Jakob Beer), who had achieved a position in Italy second only to Rossini's as a composer of Italian opera.

Meyerbeer (1791–1864) made his Paris debut with *Il crociato in Egitto*, first given in Venice on 7 March 1824. The Paris premiere was on 22 September 1825, not with Nourrit as the leading tenor, but with Donzelli, a harbinger of vocal evolution to come. Its success established Meyerbeer in Paris and paved the way for *Robert le diable* (1831) and *Les Huguenots* (1836), both built around the dramatic and vocal genius of Adolphe Nourrit.

Two others were key figures, if not exactly catalysts, in the formative years of Nourrit's career. One was the great French tragedian Talma.[4] The other, as previously noted, was Manuel García, singer and pedagogue (if the teacher only of his children, the future Maria Malibran and Pauline Viardot, and his son Manuel, Jr., and Nourrit).

Nourrit was stage-struck from an early age, and his idol in

adolescence was not a singer, but Talma. His father, as mentioned, was a singer (and diamond merchant), and there was always music in the house. Many of the family's friends were also singers.

The young Adolphe sang as a boy soprano in the choir of the family church, and at school (Sainte-Barbe) he studied violin and solfège. But his father favored a career in commerce for his son, wishing to spare him the tribulations of life in the theater. At sixteen Adolphe was apprenticed to an accountant. In his spare time he went to the theater, and, alone at home, practiced imitating the effects he had so admired there.

Accountancy lasted just eighteen months. He was then sent to Lyons to work for a silk merchant. After five or six months of that, he begged his father to bring him back to Paris. There he worked for a time as a statistician in an insurance company. At home he studied his father's arias and sang for friends on social occasions. On one such occasion, García, who happened to be visiting in an adjacent room, heard him singing an air from *Armide*. García was so impressed by what he heard that he begged Nourrit, Sr., to let him take the young man in hand.

After a few months of study, García demanded that young Adolphe give up all else and devote himself exclusively to singing. There followed eighteen months of rigorous work on fundamentals, thanks to which, subsequently, Nourrit, as a singer, could draw upon an Italianate vocal schooling to add a lyrical eloquence to the French declamatory art that was his by instinct, observation, emulation, and study.

As a student of García's, Nourrit seemed destined for a career at the Théâtre-Italien, and indeed would have preferred it, fearing to appear in his father's theater, the Opéra. But he was heard at an audition by a minister of the royal household and recommended to the Opéra. The engagement began on 27 April 1821. He became principal tenor in 1824.

In that same year he married Adèle Duverger, daughter of Alexandre Duverger, a *régisseur* at the Opéra-Comique and later a theatrical agent. We will hear much about and from her in the following pages.

Throughout all this period of study and career advancement, Nourrit continued his visits to the Théâtre-Français and to the theater magic of Talma. At the peak of his career he was called the Talma of the lyric theater, and Quicherat goes so far as to say that it was the example of Talma that made Nourrit a singer.[5]

And thus the career was launched. It is not the career, however, summarized in our preface, that most concerns us here. It is rather his last days, as told by himself in his letters to his family and friends and in their letters to him and to each other, to which we may now turn.

Part 1

FRANCE: Withdrawal from the Opéra
and Provincial Tour

Our story begins with a letter from Adolphe Nourrit, dated 19 October 1836, to a friend, Auguste Féréol, an actor and obviously the last, or one of the last, to be advised of Nourrit's decision not to renew his contract with the Opéra, but to insure his future by the takings from an extensive tour of the French provinces.

What you are about to read may well surprise you. So, in order that your surprise may not come too soon, and that your judgment of what I am about to tell you not be impaired, I shall proceed in an orderly manner: first the exposition, then the event, and finally the denouement. Don't be alarmed, and know in advance that the happiness of my family and myself is the moral of the story.

You have, perhaps, learned from the newspapers that Duprez has just been engaged by the Opéra. Do you know who he is? Possibly not. I shall tell you. Duprez is a man of talent who sang at the Odéon, a pupil of Choron's.[1] At that time he had no voice, but sang delightfully, and with musical feeling that revealed a splendid and lovely natural endowment. He has been in Italy, where, after vegetating for some years in theaters of the second and third rank, singing secondary roles, he ended by developing a colossal voice with which he achieved, I assure you, great effects. He did not become what we in France call a *bon-comédien*, but he learned sufficiently how to comport himself on the stage and how to move that one could say of him that he is a fervent actor.

Following his great success in Italy, Duprez wished to return to France, and the Opéra was the only theater that suited him. But since, in Italy, he had been No. 1, he could not consent to being No. 2 in Paris. It was necessary, therefore, that the Opéra, in order to engage him, offer him an appropriate place. One could not, however, offer him that place by merely somewhat adjusting mine. One would have to make room for him in the chair that I have occupied for the past fifteen years, and I would have to live with it.

Before signing with Duprez, Duponchel[2] advised me of his intentions. The reasons he gave me were good. He had great confidence in me, but I could fall sick, and the Opéra would have to close its doors if I were to remain a month in my bed. (I should add, in passing, that, until the present, the Opéra and I have got on well, the one supporting the other. Ask M. Véron.[3]) Here is the plan Duponchel outlined to me: In his deal with Duprez he would agree to assign to him half the new productions, the other half going to me. Each of us would take his turn. In this manner I would be less fatigued, and the Opéra would be able to sleep peacefully. And that's not all. A new work is not put on at the Opéra in a fortnight, and in order not to pay Duprez for six months of doing nothing, he must make his debut. On top of all else, I must offer all my roles and place them at his disposition. Effusive thanks from Duponchel.

That's still not all. Duprez, in order, they say, to avoid all comparison, all contention, desires that I no longer sing the role he has chosen for his debut, namely, Arnold in *William Tell*. It is a pleasure to convey to Duponchel that this is not fair. Several members of the Opéra Commission protest in my favor against this article in Duprez's contract, and it is agreed that, since I have behaved so well in the matter, Duprez should consult with me, and that nothing should be done against my wishes.

Duprez comes to see me, and after a friendly discussion, he departs, well satisfied with me. All goes well up to that point. The newspapers commend my disinterestedness, my loyalty. Even I become enthusiastic about it. I see in this rivalry a new stimulation to my love of the art. I shall owe to this competition progress that I would not, perhaps, have made in the secure position I have enjoyed for too long. In a word, I dreamt the most beautiful of all possible dreams. It was, of course, nothing but a dream. I found out when I awoke, and here's how.

The first role I had to sing after all this was Arnold. The new stimulus that I counted on did not fail me. I have never sung or acted my role as I did on this occasion. Never have I enjoyed such public acclaim, so much, indeed, that, I was told, Duprez, who was in the house, no longer wished to make his debut as Arnold (a courtesy to me, and nothing more).

The second role assigned to me was Masaniello [in *La muette de Portici*]. I knew that he had sung the role in Italian, and the same stimulant worked on me again. For a moment the excitement went to my head, and I wanted to do more than I had ever done before. I had begun to notice, too, that my family and my friends were concerned about the impending struggle, and this brought home to me the fact that my position was no longer the same. On this day of *La muette*, which I had not sung for two years, there were a lot of people who certainly had come only for me, as *La muette* has the distinction of driving away the public, the best receipts being no more than two or three thousand francs.

I had to respond to this attention, and was rather keyed up. My voice, unfortunately, was not similarly responsive, or possibly it was that a slight annoyance sufficed to leave me no longer master of my resources. Here is what happened. At my entrance, the audience let me know by its applause that it was glad to see me. But then the gentlemen of the claque (to whom, no doubt, I had been recommended injudiciously by the management out of gratitude for all I had done for them) redoubled the applause with shouts of "bravo," which indicated all too clearly their source. I blushed. I was ashamed of this absurd ovation, and said so aloud to my colleagues onstage. The effect on me was so unfortunate that for a moment I was struck by a dizzy spell that impaired my vision. When I started to sing, my middle voice was veiled. I felt that I would be unable to finish my role, and it was only with great resourcefulness that I was able to get through the act. It was impossible to continue, and [Pierre François] Wartel had to sing the last two acts.

Since then I have regained my composure, and my voice has entirely recovered. But in the meantime thoughts have been crowding in upon me. I have come to understand that my future at the Opéra will no longer be like my past, and I have drawn the following conclusions. It would be unwise to count on singing for more than another four years. Despite the raise Duponchel is offering me, I shall not be able to put aside more than a hundred thousand francs during those four years, as my expenses must always be in proportion to my income. I have always thought of retiring early enough to make a grand tour of the provinces, the income from which should not be less than a hundred thousand francs. I earned seventeen thousand in my last month. Now, will I be able to make that grand tour four years from now? Today all my repertoire is new. The operas with which I now earn money will be old and tired, and between now and then I shall be doing only half the new works given at the Opéra. Chance might have it that the operas I shall sing may not be suitable for production in the provinces. In the last five years *Robert le diable* and *La Juive* are the only two operas they have wanted from us. My regular repertoire will be passé, and it could be that between now and then I shall have no new successes. The outlook at the Opéra is not reassuring in that respect. All that without taking into account that I shall certainly have lost some of my moral fiber, if only because I will have ceased to be the first and only one, and you know how the public is drawn to the new.

You will already have guessed where I am heading. Having looked at all sides of the issue, I remain convinced that I would have nothing to gain from a struggle in which I risk losing everything, and that I should not expose myself to being only No. 2. Don't protest against my fears. I shall tell you upon what they rest.

First, by the nature of his talent, Duprez pulls the rug from under my feet, and here's how. He is not coming on the scene with youthful resources and a fresh voice, and he cannot take on roles that I have already abandoned. The strength and the power that my voice has developed over the past few years direct me to heavy roles, and it is precisely in these that Duprez's vigor is remarkable. He arrives fully sung in, fully prepared, in the path upon which I wish to set out. If each of us is to find his place, I'll find myself relegated to the cooing love birds. Thank you very much!

There's another matter, and one that will help you understand to what an extent my position is changed. They have committed themselves to Duprez to produce for him an opera by Halévy [*Guido et Ginevra*], in which the leading role had been given to me. I have already had several meetings to improve the libretto of that opera. For Halévy, who knows me and who knows all I did for him in *La Juive*, and who has been friend and advisor, to have decided to take back from me a role promised me, given to me, discussed with me, returned by me improved, Halévy, of all people, has to find in Duprez's talent the great certainty of success for his work (for, in fact, success is the only thing composers seek, and we know all that they are capable of doing in pursuit of that goal).

To finish regaling you with this matter, I must say that I see Duponchel piling idiocy upon idiocy (always with the best intentions in the world). When he took over the Opéra, all the cogs were in place, and the machine could run by itself. But now he must organize everything, for all our contracts terminate at the same time. Duponchel is incapable of a wise solution. If he is to fall on his face, I would just as soon not be there, for the artists always feel the effects of the collapse of a regime.

You may well imagine how much, under these circumstances, I have missed you. I have made a weighty decision, and I shall be happy to have your support. But since I know even your most intimate thoughts, I am confident that when I have told you of the decision I have made you will say, with my family and friends: Amen.

My contract expires in June, or even in March, if I subtract two months of leave due me. I shall have put in sixteen years of service minus one month, and am entitled to a pension after fifteen years. I have, moreover, my benefit performance, assured me upon my engagement. So, I leave the Opéra for good, and after my grand provincial tour, which I shall not terminate until I have one hundred thousand francs put aside, I shall retire and give myself over to all the studies that can open up a new career. That is three years gained for my future. Also, one must look ahead. If, after Duprez's debut, the Opéra finds that it cannot get along without me, I will be in the best of all possible positions to return. If the contrary, you will agree, it is better that I take wing in advance.

This decision has not been made without the complete approval of all my friends, approval without qualification. My wife, mother, father, brother, and sister are all happy about it, and were the first to express their approval. I do not yet have yours, but am sure that I can count on it. I have always said that, whatever my ideas about the future, I would not leave the Opéra, but that if the Opéra were to leave me, I would depart without regret. That is what I now do. I have confidence in the future. I have the courage and strength to work for it. Since making this decision, I am happier, and especially so in respect of the happiness and serenity of those about me, for it was their concern that opened my eyes to my position.[4]

Nourrit bade the Opéra farewell on 1 April 1837, with Act II of Gluck's *Armide* and the three last acts of Meyerbeer's *Les Huguenots*, the choice designed to frame a career. He had made his debut as Pylades in Gluck's *Iphigénie en Tauride* in 1821, and his last new role was Raoul in *Les Huguenots* in 1836. The farewell was a memorably emotional and successful occasion. His tour of the provinces began immediately and brilliantly with visits to Brussels, Antwerp, and

Lille. Marseilles followed in May and June, and there his troubles began. Remembering the disaster in *La muette de Portici*, recounted in his letter to Féréol, it might be more accurate to say that they recurred.

He arrived on 14 May to be overwhelmed by the warmth of his welcome, the frigidity of a Marseilles May, and the intensity of the famous and infamous mistral. Returning to Paris from Brussels, Antwerp, and Lille, he had experienced trouble with his throat, and later reproached himself for not having taken a longer rest before setting off to Marseilles. His indisposition never left him entirely during his five weeks in the Midi, in the course of which, after a successful debut as Arnold in *William Tell*, he appeared in *Robert le diable, La muette de Portici,* Boieldieu's *La dame blanche*, Rossini's *Le Comte Ory*, and Pierre Gaveaux's *Le bouffe et le tailleur*. Indeed, his problems gradually grew worse, and led to another disaster during a performance of *La Juive* on 13 June when, in Act IV, his voice failed him completely.

Nourrit's own account of that evening, in a letter to his wife dated 15 June, is a curious mixture of fact and glossing over, designed partly to spare his wife and partly to spare and reassure himself.

You must have been anxious to find out how *La Juive* went. But since Eugène [Duverger, his brother-in-law] gets *Le Sémaphore* you probably have heard from him the effect produced by the second act. It was tremendous, so tremendous that nothing like it has ever before been seen in Marseilles. The third act was very good, too. The beautiful line I sing in the finale was sensational. Then, in the fourth act, the duet with the Cardinal also went very well. But just when I started to sing my aria ["Rachel, quand du Seigneur"], I was seized with a violent hoarseness, so severe that I thought I would not be able to finish. I made a tremendous effort, however, and had enough will to get to the end, but only by forcing my voice. You can imagine what condition I was in at the end. I had only a few words to sing in the fifth act, and managed to do it.

But although I was displeased with my performance, the same cannot be said of the audience, which was charming, and seemed to want me to understand that it realized I had suddenly been stricken with an affliction brought on by the heat wave. I won't tell you all the silly, crazy things that went through my head after this misfortune. Now that I am calmer, I either laugh at myself or am ashamed.[5]

The distressing events that occurred during that fateful performance of *La Juive* are more vividly and accurately detailed in a letter written to the editor of the *Revue Musicale* shortly after Nourrit's suicide by M. G. Bénédit, "laureate de notre Conservatoire dans la classe de déclamation et professeur de chant au Conservatoire de Marseille" (laureate of our Conservatory in declamation and professor of song at the Marseilles Conservatory). The letter, dated 25 April 1839, was published in the issue of the same date:

Gripped by a disastrous hoarseness, Nourrit had struggled valiantly through three acts. Then, at the moment of his great aria, "Rachel, quand du Seigneur," fatigue, fear, and emotion completely paralyzed his voice. That voice, heretofore enjoying so wide a range, whose pure and vibrant notes in the upper octave had such great power and charm, was barely able to reach to F. Reduced to these feeble resources, Nourrit, thanks to his admirable intelligence, was still able to marshal sufficient means to finish the allegro. But having reached that point, his strength gave out at the last measure and, despite incredible effort to reach the piercing A-flat which ends the aria on the tonic, he was obliged for the first time to sing an octave lower "la couronne du martyr!"

Pale and trembling with grief, he put his hand to his forehead, made a gesture of despair, and left the stage in a state of unspeakable agitation. Fearing the dire effect of such a collapse upon Nourrit, whose constant companion I had been since his arrival in Marseilles, I dashed from my seat and, heading for the corridor leading to the wings, I reached his dressing room at the same time as M. Xavier Boisselot [1816–1893, a local composer and piano manufacturer whose songs Nourrit had sung privately at Marseilles]. Alas! No doubt about it. Our poor artist had gone mad!

Never in my life shall I forget that frightful scene. His eyes aflame, his countenance wild, Nourrit was stomping around, striking the walls, uttering heart-rending sobs. In this awful state he was unable to recognize us.

"Who are you? What do you want with me? Leave me alone!"

"They are friends of yours who have come to see you."

"Friends of mine? Impossible—If you are my friends, kill me—Don't you see that I can't live any longer, that I am done for, dishonored?"

Upon uttering these words, he made a violent lunge toward the window. We jumped on him, seizing him with all our might, and dragged him to an armchair where, overcome by the one-sided struggle, he collapsed without further resistance in deep dejection. The crisis lasted a long time. Restored to his senses through the care of Dr. Forcade, who had joined us in this grievous episode, Nourrit opened his eyes, and seeing the silent consternation all around him, asked our pardon with all the ingenuousness and timidity of a child who has just made a blunder. We took advantage of this momentary reaction to urge him to return to the stage. He consented resignedly. The audience, informed of what had transpired during the intermission, gave him its enthusiastic applause. At the end of the performance we took our friend back to the Hôtel de la Darse. After calming him, we left, promising to return the next day.[6]

In Marseilles Nourrit sang only once again, at a private gathering in the salon of Boisselot. He sang well, but felt obliged to forgo a duet from *William Tell* that he was to have sung with his friend Bénédit. "Imagine," he said to Bénédit, "I who have never had to change a number in all my life being reduced to backing out on a duet. O my God, I feel that it is all over for me."[7]

Suffering from persistent dysentery, Nourrit canceled two remaining performances of *La muette de Portici* and left Marseilles the evening of 22 June. He arrived home in Paris "his skin livid, his cheeks hollow, his eyes lustreless, his manner crestfallen," according to one witness. "One would never have believed that such a physical change could have taken place in such a short time."[8]

Two weeks of rest and care brought apparent recovery, and Nourrit resumed his tour, this time accompanied by his wife. In Lyons in July and August he sang fifteen performances of *La Juive, William Tell, Les Huguenots, La muette de Portici, Robert le diable*, Spontini's *Fernand Cortez*, and Auber's *Le philtre*, including six performances of *Les Huguenots*. All went well, and he had an enormous triumph. It was at Lyons, his wife later wrote to a friend, that Nourrit enjoyed his last days of success.[9]

At the end of August, he and his wife continued on to Toulouse. His digestive ailments, now more violent and prolonged, recurred and laid him low for a fortnight. He was eventually able to fulfill his engagements, but the recovery was only temporary. "Adolphe," his wife wrote to a friend, "although better, is coughing again, especially at night, and there are moments when he says: 'I shall never recover here. I am sick. I feel it.'"[10]

His engagement at Bordeaux had to be canceled, although his presence in the city as a visitor was appropriately honored, most notably by a banquet where the orchestra and artists of the Grand Théâtre serenaded him with excerpts from the operas with which he had been most prominently and affectionately associated.

Back in Paris at the end of October, he continued to suffer from deteriorating health and surrendered to a severe course of medical treatment. The results were promising for a time, and he prepared to resume his provincial Odyssey. It was not to be. What happened then, precipitating him upon a far more fateful Odyssey in Italy, and the reasoning that lay behind a momentous decision, are related in his own words, again in a letter to his friend Féréol, dated 22 November 1837:

I was all packed and ready to take off again for the provinces. I wasn't even worried about the cough I was getting, nor another problem [presumably digestive] that has persisted despite treatment and precautions. Then another really bad cold got hold of me, and that was that. M. Louis [his physician] took the matter very seriously, and dosed me up solidly in order to get rid of both the cold and the colic. Thus, I have spent the last two weeks by the fireside, taking barley water, sulphur water, pills, potions, and enemas. I have even treated myself to some fifteen leech applications and one vesication [blistering of the abdomen]. But my condition remains about the same. . . . This sickness would have been an annoyance under any circumstances, since it means the loss of much-needed income. But when I tell you of my latest decision, my hopes, and my plans, you will see that all is for the best in the best of all possible worlds.

In my last letter I told you of my first impression of Duprez in *La muette de Portici*. I have since seen him in *Les Huguenots* and *William Tell*. I have not heard him in *La Juive*. Without doubt, for a certain endowment, either vocal or dramatic, the Opéra is too big. Vocal subtleties are lost beyond the first row of the parterre. Delicacies of inflection pass unnoticed, and facial expressions cannot be seen. I had already assumed as much, and now my assumptions are confirmed. Therefore, whatever happens, I am more determined than ever never to return to the Opéra.

I must now tell you of another effect Duprez has had on

me, and an important one. Do you know the first words I uttered after I last heard Duprez? "I must go to Italy!" I spent the whole night thinking about it, and reached the decision more willingly since I have been fighting the idea for ten years, and have had ample opportunity to weigh the disadvantages as well as the advantages, and I hope that you will approve the reason that has brought me to it.

First, I must tell you that this decision has been welcomed joyously by everyone in my family. It had long been their secret wish. Proud of me as they are, prouder, indeed, than I of myself, all my triumphs in the provinces left them only half satisfied. They wanted to see me successful in a greater, more exalted, career. . . . Perhaps you, too, have felt the same, and have hesitated to say so. In any case, here are my reasons:

To begin with, you may well have surmised that this business of running around the provinces is intolerable for me. Traveling with my children is impossible, traveling alone very painful, and all that in order to do rather poor business. The money I earn is insufficient compensation for all the trouble. I thought for a while that my presence and advice could improve musical performances in the places I visited. Illusion! My efforts have succeeded only in tiring me out, costing me money, and causing annoyance to those whom I had hoped to help in ridding themselves of their bad habits. The theaters are even sicker in the provinces than in Paris.

Should I return to Paris and accept the proposals of the Opéra-Comique (which are superb)? Many have advised me to do so. But I haven't the slightest appetite for it. I would be putting myself in a worse position than the one I left. I think there are great opportunities for me at the Opéra. It is becoming more disorganized every day, and the vogue of Duprez is declining. His voice is showing signs of fatigue, and the composers who supported him at first, now seeing that they are being held responsible for the weak effect he achieves in their works, would all, I am sure, come back to me. But, I repeat, I have no appetite for it.

That is what is influencing my decision to go to Italy. Rubini is retiring next year, and the position of first tenor in Italy will be open. I propose to pursue it. Through studies I have made of the Italian style, I have become convinced that with so sonorous and musical a language, my voice should increase in intensity, volume, and suppleness.

I am departing, moreover, only with the wish to discover for myself the state of the theaters, the state of the public, and the opportunities open to me. When I have visited the principal cities and heard the best works and the best artists, I shall make my final decision. . . . Until now, Italy has been for me a sort of fearsome phantom. Now I must see it face to face, and then, perhaps, I shall no longer be afraid of it.

In any case, the trip can only do me good. The doctors favor it as a means of getting rid of the cough which has plagued me now for two months. Since they advise a winter of rest, this seems a good way of spending it without tiring my voice. . . .

So, it is a well-considered decision. As soon as the doctors allow it, I shall pack and leave without saying anything to anyone. I want to avoid gossip, rumors, *if*s and *but*s. Not until I am in Rome or Naples do I want people to know that I have gone to Italy. Another reason for leaving that I haven't told you: I have found an excellent traveling companion, my cousin Barthélemy, traveler par excellence, a Wandering Jew. With him I shall be sure to see all the nooks and crannies of Italy without the usual tourist troubles.

Well, my dear friend! There is something new, something to think about! For the moment, however, it is nothing but a pleasure trip, a way of not wasting completely the two months of rest that have been prescribed. Since I have decided upon this course of acton, I am completely at peace with myself. I have regained my courage, and I see the future more clearly. With Italian, my resources will be greater, and I shall have all Europe to exploit. . . .

Until now, I have been known as a good actor who can sing. I want to try now to be a perfect singer as well as a good actor.[11]

Part 2

ITALY: Turin, Genoa, Milan, Venice, Florence, Rome, Naples

Nourrit was to remain in Paris another month. His first stop in Italy was Turin, where he and his cousin arrived on 26 December. There, and subsequently in Genoa, as we learn from his letters to his wife, he devoted himself to sight-seeing and theater-going. He was unimpressed by what he heard at the opera (yelling), but better pleased by the spoken theater and pantomime. What he says of a tenor (unidentified) at the Carlo Felice in Genoa is worth passing on for what it has to say about style:

I can't say that he yells, but neither can I say that he sings well, for where there are no nuances there is no singing. And then it seemed to me that his voice is under-employed, for he didn't try a single ornament. It appears that ornamentation is completely out of style here. They now sing only the notes. They don't even take the trouble to change or embellish the theme a little at the repeats.[1]

Also worth noting is Nourrit's account of a meeting with the baritone Giovanni Inchindi, who had sung in Paris at the Opéra-Comique:

He was very surprised to see me in Italy. . . . He doesn't understand my actions, and still thinks I did a foolish thing to leave the Opéra. I took good care not to let him in on my plans. For him, as for everyone else, this is nothing but a pleasure trip. He asked me confidentially if I shall be singing in Italy. I assured him that nothing was farther from my mind, and he expressed his approval. His opinion is not of the slightest importance to me. If he cannot understand my leaving the Opéra, how could he understand my making a debut in Italy?[2]

There could be no similar dissimulation in Milan, where he arrived on 10 January 1838. His first visit was to Rossini, to whom, of course, he was well and affectionately known as the creator of the roles of Néoclès in *Le siège de Corinthe*, Aménophis in *Moïse*, the Comte Ory, and Arnold. As he wrote to his wife on the evening of his arrival:

I got dressed and went immediately to Rossini's. He wasn't home. I tried again, and am already well pleased with this first visit. I put my cards right on the table, and I'll try to repeat his exact words:

"Never has the moment been better for you, and that is not paying you a compliment. You will see for yourself that there is no singer of talent in Italy. It is now no longer a matter of doing roulades, and the facility of a Rubini would not stand him in good stead today. What is wanted is expression and declamation. So there is no need to waste your time in unnecessary work. I approve of your trip to Italy in every way. Only, when you have made up your mind, you must tell me so, for then we will need to carry on a bit of diplomacy."[3]

In Milan Nourrit could not be the anonymous tourist he had been in Turin and Genoa. "Here we are in Milan," he wrote to his wife on 12 January, "where I know a number of people: Rossini, [Ferdinand] Hiller,[4] [Johann Peter] Pixis[5] and his [adopted] daughter [Francilla, a successful contralto], Mme [Giuditta] Pasta,[6] and Dérancourt and his wife [Desiderata, a soprano]. Soon all Milan knew about me. Invitations, politeness on all sides. . . . As a result, ever since my arrival I have had no time to myself. . . . Liszt arrived yesterday, and he has already called on me once. I had to dine with him and Hiller."[7]

Of a subsequent dinner meeting with Rossini, Nourrit reported in his letter to his wife of 12 January:

I told him that since he thought this a good moment for me to launch myself in Italy, I would hesitate no longer, and leave it to him as to how I should proceed. He thinks I should continue my travels. "You must know Italy well," he told me. "You must nationalize yourself. I will give you good letters for the cities you will be visiting. But in order to begin making good use of your time, you must take along one or two roles and learn them as you go along. I recommend *Lucia*. It is the best among modern operas. . . ."

And here is something else. Today Rossini is giving his last musical evening,[8] and he wants me to sing. I resisted at first, all the while agreeing to do whatever he desired. I will not be announced, but it is agreed that I'll have to be coaxed, and that after looking about for a piece palatable to the Milanese, I shall sing the duet with baritone from *William Tell*

["Où vas-tu" from Act I]. I rehearsed it yesterday at Hiller's apartment, then sang it this morning with Rossini. I think I am in good voice. Hiller and Liszt, who would like to see me stay in Italy, are happy that I am singing this evening before the cream of the Milanese public. You can imagine my excitement. It is just about the same for me as a first performance.[9]

Very much later that night he was to write:

It's almost one o'clock, but I don't wish to go to bed before telling you of my success this evening. It surpassed all that I could have hoped for. I won't speak of my agitation. It was extreme. They said I had a frightening pallor, and the warm reception of the entire audience when they saw me approach the piano only increased my nervousness. Despite all that, it appears that I sang well, and it may be that my nervousness even helped me. As it was, they didn't let me finish the repeat of the duet, and four measures before the end they began to shout in such a way that I could have left off singing. . . . At the end of the duet the noise went on for a quarter of an hour. . . . It was one of my best evenings, a good start, but I want to leave it at that for the moment, and depart soon in order not to let this first impression become diluted and weakened by repeats that could never have that burst of enthusiasm that a first hearing alone can produce. It was a good seed. We shall let it bear its fruits.[10]

Nourrit's duet that evening was followed by Liszt improvising on themes from *William Tell*. The next day, again in a letter to his wife, he wrote:

I have just seen Rossini again. He is of the opinion that I should leave Milan soon. He wants me to get through my Italian tour quickly so that I can make my debut in the spring. I suggested that it might be better to wait until the autumn, but he thinks that would serve no purpose. We shall see. The most important thing is the choice of theater, opera, and, above all, the company. I spoke to him of making my debut in Milan. "See all Italy first," he said, "then make your choice."

My success at Rossini's is the talk of the town. Everyone thinks that the director of La Scala is going to engage me. . . . People vie with one another to invite me. They bother Rossini in the best of houses to introduce me there. Rossini has been kind enough to put them off, and a fictitious cold has spared me many invitations whose objective was to have me sing. Since I am not yet ready to sing in Italian, I don't wish to sing a word of French under any pretext. . . .

Meanwhile, I have booked tickets for Venice for tomorrow. I can't wait to get away from Milan. If the authorities want to get in touch with me, they will know where to write, and, in any case, I am content to see something of the rest of Italy before deciding what will be best for me. Not that I have anything against Milan, least of all after the hit I made at Rossini's. Among the nice things that are being said of me, this is the nicest: "Not since [Maria] Malibran has anyone experienced a greater musical sensation than that produced by the duet from *William Tell*." So my mind is now made up, and I am entering bravely upon my new career. I shall not draw back from the first opportunity to reaffirm it irrevocably.[11]

Nourrit, accompanied by Hiller, arrived in Venice on 22 January to find the canals frozen and the gondoliers breaking ice with their oars. "I hardly expected to come to Venice," he wrote, "to make my first journey on ice."[12] His stay there coincided with the rehearsal and premiere (30 January) of Donizetti's *Maria de Rudenz*. He was thus afforded the opportunity to meet not only the composer, but also Caroline Ungher,[13] who sang the title role, and the great baritone Giorgio Ronconi,[14] who sang the role of Corrado.

He wrote to his wife in a letter dated 23 January:

Last night after dinner Hiller took me to the house of Mme Ungher, the prima donna who was with us for one season in Paris [1833–34]. Needless to say, she received me very cordially. In Paris she had always shown a high regard for me and my singing. . . . She took us to the dress rehearsal of the last two acts of Donizetti's opera. This rehearsal was more interesting for me than all the performances in the world, and now I know one more side of the theaters in Italy. Donizetti, when he saw me, embraced me warmly and introduced me with great compliments to the principals and to the director, who received me very well. . . .

There is nothing very new in what we heard, but it is music that will probably please the public and have a good success [it was withdrawn after two performances]. The company seems to me the best of any I have yet encountered. There is a baritone named Ronconi who has a delightful and sometimes robust voice. He sings well and is probably an intelligent actor. As for Mme Ungher, she really sings very inspiringly at times. Her voice is not great, but she achieves great heights of passion. Despite her failings, I can understand her popularity with the public.

I paid my compliments to all these people, trying to find in my Italian the most gracious expressions available to me. I also congratulated the director on his beautiful theater [La Fenice, opened in 1792] and on his excellent company. During the rehearsal he came and sat down next to me, and several times urged me not to leave Italy. Was it simply courtesy? Was it to sound me out? I don't know. In any case, I did not give myself away. For all these people I want to be merely an amateur making his tour of Italy as the English do.

After the rehearsal Donizetti took us to a café and then home. He suggested that he go with me as far as Florence. His opera, which was to be performed Saturday, will not be ready until Monday, which will prolong my stay here beyond what I had intended. For myself, I shall not regret this."[15]

During the remainder of his sojourn in Venice, Nourrit did, indeed, play the tourist, taking in the sights and enjoying the hospitality accorded him as a visiting celebrity loaded down with letters of introduction to those in high places. His letters to his wife deal mostly with sight-seeing and social entertainment, but the following, from a letter dated 25 January, is worth quoting for the light it throws on the character and quality of singing in Italy at that time as heard by a French master.

Now I come to what has been the object of my journey: the theaters and music. Day before yesterday I took in a new opera, *Rosamunde* [*in Ravenna*], by a young maestro [Giuseppe Lillo (1814–1863)] for whom it is a first attempt [it was his fourth]. There is nothing in this work, not even one of those easy cantilenas that the Italians dash off almost effortlessly. The singers didn't all measure up to what I had expected from them after the rehearsal the night before. I exclude the tenor [Napoleone Moriani[16]]. He is not, strictly speaking, a great artist, but he has a beautiful voice, wide range, expressiveness, and a lot of good will. Unfortunately, he has only two colors at his disposal, black and white. I was greatly pleased with him yesterday in Rubini's role [Arturo] in *I Puritani*. He sang the last phrase well, and hit his F-sharp [above high C][17] with a delightfully fresh head tone. If only Rubini had that instrument! Aside from that, he is a young man not yet thirty, who is beginning late, so it is possible that he may become a singer of the first order.

Ronconi, the baritone who had so pleased me the night before, forces his voice too much. He shouts almost continuously, and it is only rarely that he uses his mezza voce, which I find charming and mellow. In Mme Ungher I found all the good qualities that I had already admired. But in the theater, that is to say, before the public, her failings are magnified. She often exaggerates, and when the dynamics call for full voice, she is much too shrill. But how can one blame these artists for yelling? It is the only way they can make an impression. It remains to be seen whom one should blame, the artists or the public. We shall see![18]

As for the remainder of Nourrit's stay in Venice, only one episode is worth passing on to opera-lovers and students of opera history. He was invited to a private party at the home of an amateur, Signor Perrucchini, where he sang some Schubert with Ungher with great success. He had been excited by the assurance that among a small group would be Giovanni-Battista Velluti,[19] the last of the operatic castrati, then nearing sixty. As it turned out, Velluti was indisposed and declined to sing. But, as Nourrit wrote in a letter to his wife dated 30 January,

Yesterday morning at M. Perrucchini's, [Velluti] sat down at the piano and performed a little Venetian barcarolle which he varied tastefully. He sang this with a method that you can imagine by recalling [Benedetta Rosamunda] Pisaroni and Pasta and the best of Mme [Fanny Tacchinardi-] Persiani [the first Lucia]. He is, indeed, the master of all the great singers of this period, the tree which has produced all this fine fruit. I was delighted, and it was not a banal compliment

I gave him when I said that I had just had a great lesson, and hoped never to forget it.[20]

Nourrit arrived in Florence on 5 February accompanied by Donizetti, Hiller, and his cousin, after experiencing the usual vicissitudes, adventures, misadventures, and travails of coach travel across the Appenines at that time of year. Awaiting him he found a package of letters from his wife and other members of his family. These missives disturbed him and prompted him to respond:

My joy should not, perhaps, be unmixed, for I can see that you are worried, and from the little you tell me of what worries you, I can guess the sadness filling the moments you could be spending with me. Poor dear! . . . But my head is also beginning to be troubled by the thought of that happiness we all had when we were together. And to think that we could still have had that happiness if I had had a little more energy, a little more confidence in myself, if I had not left my position.

Ah! I need to forget in order not to lose my courage. I must keep before my eyes only the future that unfolds before me. This future can be glorious, and full of happiness, too! So forgive me for the difficulties to which I shall have exposed you in order to procure it. I share all your trials and tribulations, as you will know without my saying so.

Despite everything, I don't regret what I have done. I feel strong enough to carry out the task I have set myself, and I will undergo anything in order to reach my goal. . . . I accept with confidence everything that happens to me, and since what I want is good, and I want it resolutely, I firmly believe that anything that doesn't work out according to my wishes of the moment is ordained by a will that guides me ever more surely toward my goal.[21]

Nourrit continued on to Pisa and Livorno, and from Livorno to Rome by sea, still playing the tourist. Even from Rome his letters tell of little but sight-seeing and social entertainment. But on the eve of his departure for Naples, his ultimate destination, he received a letter from Rossini. The latter, in Milan, had promised to assist Nourrit in any way possible, and in Venice and Florence the tenor had awaited word, keeping in mind Rossini's advice to complete his tour and become acquainted with Italy, and never pressing the composer for news. Rossini's letter, which Nourrit translated into French for his wife in a letter dated 1 March 1838, was as follows (here translated from the French):

"Several days ago, I was requested by [Bartolomeo] Merelli [impresario of La Scala] and the Count P. [Latka, secretary to the governor] to offer you an engagement in Milan for two consecutive seasons, specifically, the autumn and the following carnival season, with the understanding that you will be in Milan on 1 August 1838 and stay there until 30 March 1839. For your debut you will have an opera written especially for you, or even an opera of your choice. There remains only the fee (if the contract and its duration suit you). For the two seasons I would ask 50,000 zwanzigs (the zwanzig is worth about 85 centimes in France). You can do what seems best to you. Answer with a letter that can be used as a contractual document, so that if your proposals are acceptable, I shall be in a position to sign for you. This is a favorable and glorious opportunity, and I shall be happy to be instrumental in your new career, as I am to remain yours, etc."

This [Nourrit wrote to his wife] is something definite and clear. The next step is up to me. I have to make up my mind. As you may imagine, I was rather excited when I read this letter, and I am sure that you yourself and all the family will be excited when you read it. The conditions seem favorable to me, and perhaps better than anything I could have hoped for. (True, they are not what I am being offered, but what Rossini advises me to ask.) I am persuaded that I should accept them. Since, however, I am setting out tomorrow, I think it wise to wait until I am in Naples before replying to Rossini.

He wants me to send a letter he can show, a contractual letter, so it has to be carefully thought out, and two days of reflection are none too many to draw up the accessory conditions, which are often just as important as the main ones. . . . Here I am launched on my career! When I leave Rome I say good-bye to sight-seeing and the other pleasures of being a gentleman of leisure. I am going to immerse myself from head to toe in Italian, and if I can find in Naples a place to live with an Italian family where no one knows any French, I shall not hesitate to renounce the easier life of a furnished hotel room.[22]

Part 3

ITALY: The Student (Donizetti and
the Preparation of *Poliuto*)

What Nourrit's new life and routine would entail is recounted in the singer's first letter to his wife from Naples, dated 6 March 1838:

Today I am answering Rossini in accordance with his instructions. Since the accessory conditions I have added are reasonable, I have no doubt that the matter will soon be settled. When I say "soon," I should add that I shan't have an answer from Rossini for two or three weeks, and news of the settlement of my engagement is unlikely to reach you in less than a month.

Yesterday I started work with Donizetti, and you may form your own judgment of the steps I have taken on the road to confidence and progress when I tell you that I did with him what I have never done, and would never do, with the French composers to whom I am best known and in whom I have the most confidence. I sight-read for him one of his pieces, singing in full voice and giving it all the expression I could, obliged as I was to concern myself with the notes, the musical phrasing, the meaning of the words, the pronunciation, and the accent. I settled right down to the role of pupil, and now, having started out on that basis, I can say that I am quite pleased with myself.

I am free to go forward. I have burned my bridges. I have forgotten my glorious past, my position as professor, my reputation as top French singer. I am beginning my career all over again. I am studying like one who has everything to learn. In order to get a marshal's baton you have to wear woolen epaulettes and carry a general-issue rifle. What I already know will come out later, and the public may perceive that I am embarked on my new career from a higher point of departure than others.

I told you I was pleased with Donizetti because he doesn't pay me any compliments. Anyone else might think that he doesn't pay me enough. But I like him as he is. He hasn't hidden from me the difficulties I must overcome to become an Italian singer, but he has given me the means of overcoming them, and the lesson I had yesterday will bear its fruit. I should add that after this first trial he thought my progress would be fast, and that in a short time I would be ready to sing one or two of his roles in such a way as to persuade everyone that I am a true Italian.

While I was singing, a friend [of Donizetti's] arrived. We kept on, he correcting, I working (would I ever have done that in France?). The friend took me for an Italian. Donizetti doesn't let anything get by, not even in matters of dramatic interpretation. He corrects me particularly on my nasal sounds, and I think that from every point of view I shall find his advice good. Now I am impatient to get settled in order to be able to work well. I don't want to stay in the hotel, and shall try to find a furnished apartment in a completely Italian household where no one knows a word of French. I have already selected my language teachers, and as soon as I have a piano I shall spend one or two hours every morning with an accompanist, except for the eight days of Holy Week, which I still intend to spend in Rome (if I don't have any good reason not to). I don't want to leave Naples until I know three Italian roles in such a way as to be able to sing them on short notice. Donizetti has offered to have me go over several parts by Bellini when he is satisfied with me in two of his own. . . . I'll wait to decide whether I should accept.

Barbaja [impresario of the San Carlo in Naples][1] also gave me a cordial welcome. He has opened the theater to me, and has already suggested having me sing. My word! When I'm ready, if I have the time, I shall not say no. But let's wait and see.[2]

Later, Nourrit wrote:

I have just found a place to live in the city, pleasant, nicely furnished, centrally located, and very clean—which is unusual in Naples. My cousin will share it with me until his departure for Rome, after which he will return to France, I to [remain in] Naples.

Keep yourself in readiness two months from now so that there may be no obstacles on your end to our reunion. Naples is very beautiful, and if I shall have had a successful debut, it would be wonderful to spend two months of summer with

you and the children. But let's not build castles in the air!
Let's be sensible, and leave things in the hands of God![3]

A letter of 10 March 1838 gives this account of Nourrit's
daily routine as he settled into his new role of student in
Naples:

Now my travels are over. I am beginning to change my occu-
pation. No longer am I that stroller, full of curiosity, that
tourist spending the whole day sight-seeing and visiting. I
hardly know three streets in Naples. I know where Donizetti
lives. I know the theater, and I know the seashore, where I go
to rest and enjoy the most wonderful view imaginable. When
you can have such a tableau before your eyes, what is to be
seen within four walls, even were they built of gold and precious stones? So, I leave it to my cousin to visit all the
churches.

I visit my Italian teacher every morning, and I don't stop
singing until I am tired. I have not, however, been in very
good voice. I have been bothered by a head cold which ren-
ders doubly difficult my task of correcting my nasal sounds.
Be that as it may, I keep at it, and when Donizetti feels like
giving me an hour, I take advantage of it whether I am well
disposed, rested, or tired. My whole life now is singing. Even
in the street, when I hear one of those Italian inflections that
are as melodious as music itself, I latch onto it in passing,
and repeat it twenty times until I get it right. That often
makes me look like a madman, and my cousin thinks I must

be a bit addled to be thus talking to myself when I could be conversing with him.[4]

A letter of 17 March 1838 gives these details of the singer's work with Donizetti:

A lesson, with all that the word implies! In spite of the progress he sees me making, he criticized me, yesterday, at almost every word and every note, and I can assure you that each of his observations hit the mark. Thanks to him, I shall soon be rid of a fault that has often been held against me, and that has persisted in my singing in French, namely, sometimes singing through my nose. Our language is full of nasal syllables, and rather than sacrifice the word, I have sacrificed the quality of tone. It is quite another matter in Italian—indeed, completely the reverse. The better one pronounces Italian, the better the vocal sound, and when I happen to produce a bad sound, it is because I am giving it with a French accent. As soon as I succeed in reproducing the Italian accent, my voice is entirely different. The only problem is that it tires me. Mme [Manuel] García was right when she spoke of needing three or four months to correct the faults to which our harmonious language has accustomed us.[5]

Much in Nourrit's letters at this time is devoted to the prospect of his wife's joining him in Italy. They both had misgivings, arising principally from concern over the effect upon her of the stress of travel and the change of climate. She, their six children, and her brother eventually joined him in Naples on 10 June.

Meanwhile, Nourrit passed up the Holy Week visit to Rome, preferring to remain in Naples and continue his studies with Donizetti while awaiting a reply from Milan to his own response to the contractual offer forwarded by Rossini.

In a letter to his wife of 20 March, he praised the Neapolitan climate, then continued:

Furthermore, the presence of Donizetti makes me wish to continue my work here. And then, too, if there is a possibility of my appearing under suitable circumstances in Italy before the autumn season, that could only be in Naples. Everyone here wants to hear me, but I refuse all invitations, since I don't wish to sing anything but Italian, and I don't think that I am quite ready. . . . Barbaja keeps dropping little hints to me in passing. Day before yesterday, he proposed an appearance in *William Tell*. Well, I didn't say no. But I would have to make a completely new study of the role, and today it would be harder for me to sing in Italian than some other role that I had never sung. When I am very sure of *Lucia*, I'll see about working on that one. If it suits me as well in Italian as in French, I may accept Barbaja's offer. But let's wait until the time is ripe.[6]

A postscript to this letter tells of an unexpected visitor:

I am opening my letter again to tell you of the pleasure I have just had from a visitor I was far from expecting. It was [Girolamo] Crescentini,[7] the patriarch of singers, who took the trouble to come up my three flights of stairs. I had gone to the

Conservatory [where Crescentini was teaching] to greet him, and, not finding him in, left my card. How surprised I was to see this venerable gentleman enter. He was perfectly charming to me. He remembers my father, and spoke a lot about him.[8]

A package of letters from Paris brought news of the Opéra and prompted this response in a letter to his wife dated 24 March:

I must say that the concerns of the Opéra have very little interest for me today. My life is so remote from that world that it is almost as if it didn't exist. Paris, for me, is you, my family, and those who still think of me. As for the rest, I truly can't be bothered, and I assure you that I say this dispassionately. I can no longer imagine myself in Paris, and much would have to happen to make me want to go back there in the near future.

Don't tell this to your father or my mother. Although Donizetti keeps encouraging me more and more, it is always with an eye to the effect my Italian successes will have in Paris, while for myself I am concerned only with Italy. Singing Italian is no longer a means for me to get on elsewhere. It is an end toward which all my efforts are directed. I am daily more pleased with Donizetti. Now he wants me to come to his house every day, and often it is only to make me repeat the same phrase twenty times in a row. This work is rather tiring, but once I have conquered these first difficulties of accent, I am sure that I will move along rapidly. I must say that each day I notice some progress. Is it not already an immense step forward to have learned one's faults and to know how to correct them? . . .

Duprez has probably done me quite a favor by driving me out of the Opéra and into Italy, so I should wish him well and applaud his successes like everyone else. . . . I must leave you for the moment. The time for my lesson with Donizetti has almost arrived, and I don't want to miss it. Good-bye.[9]

Later, Nourrit wrote to his wife:

I hope very much that when you hear me it will be easy for you to see that I have not wasted my time. But don't be surprised at a change which may not please you at first. I have had to put aside certain qualities to which we are very attached in France, and which are not desired in Italy. We sing the way we speak, with our lips taut and a certain restraint which in France is considered good form. Here everything is on the surface, everything is sonorous, everything is music, even the language.

At first I still retained that French reserve which, to tell the truth, cost me half my resources. For fear of going too far, I didn't go far enough. Today I am no longer afraid, whether in speaking or singing, to indulge in that abundance of accentuation which really has great power. My ear has already grown so accustomed to it that it is unpleasant for me to hear a Frenchman speak Italian. I myself stop short when I sense that I am falling back into old habits. I still don't speak Italian with the same ease as I speak French, but I can say that nothing bothers me. As for accent, I sometimes deceive Italian ears, especially when I don't have a long conversation to maintain (because in long phrases, gallicisms give away my origin). Sometimes, in the evening, I find myself tired by this continual concentration. But a walk beside the sea and a good night's sleep restore me quickly.[10]

In a letter to his wife of 30 March, Nourrit reports on an excursion to Pompeii, in the course of which he caught a cold and missed two lessons with Donizetti. The letter continues with a first reference to a matter that was to have momentous consequences for both the composer and the singer in the months to come.

He [Donizetti] is negotiating with the Théâtre-Italien in Paris, which has asked him for an opera for next winter, and he has consulted with me on the choice of a subject. In the course of discussion we fell upon an idea which pleased him, and he urged me to write a scenario for him, suitable for setting to music and bearing in mind the available singers and their capabilities. I spent all last evening and several hours this morning constructing the plan for an opera in three acts, which I am taking to him today.[11]

The subject was Corneille's *Polyeucte*. Nourrit's draft scenario would be crafted into an Italian libretto as *Poliuto* by Salvatore Cammarano and set to music by Donizetti as a vehicle for Nourrit in the title role. Although the opera was completed and even rehearsed at the San Carlo, the Bourbon censors objected to the religious implications of the subject, and banned it. It was subsequently set in French by Scribe, and became *Les martyrs*, first performed at the Opéra on 10 April 1840, with Duprez in the title role.[12]

The same letter of 30 March foresaw the collapse of Nourrit's negotiations, through Rossini, with La Scala in Milan.

I was expecting Rossini's answer today. . . . I doubt that it can be worked out. According to what theater people tell me, the breach-of-contract clause in case of cholera makes it impossible. The governments of Italy would not permit such a condition, which would inevitably bring about the closing of the theaters, and that would be a public calamity greater than the epidemic. I think that Barbaja is waiting for this affair to collapse in order to make his offer to me. He has no one for the autumn season, and his son has already spoken to me about it. Thus, no worry. We'll follow the road that opens up before us, trusting in God, who knows our aim and wishes.[13]

Nourrit's letter of 4 April to his wife records Rossini's answer and its consequences.

My proposals were accepted only with many restrictions by Merelli, the director of La Scala, and these restrictions are such that I am refusing the engagement. (Let me say right away that I am in no way angry about this, and that I even have more than one reason to be happy about it. You will soon be convinced of that.) Merelli grants me only forty thousand Austrian pounds, and he wants me to sing *opera buffa*. What he needs with Donzelli is a *tenore sfogato* (*ténor léger*, as we say in France), and in me he hasn't found his man. And then, he gives me no assurance of the choice for my debut. He offers *Le Comte Ory*. It was hardly worth going to the trouble! As for Donizetti or Mercadante, I can't count on them for the opera that would be written for me. He [Merelli] has made contracts with other masters. Then—well, there is nothing acceptable in the whole thing. Rossini's letter reassures me by anticipating the reasons why I should not accept the arrangement. He even tells me: "If they offer you an engagement in Naples, take it." That is clear enough. So I didn't hesitate. My reply went off yesterday. I refused categorically. Now I can't even be sorry about the matter.

I have already told you that Barbaja has proposed several times to have me make my debut at the San Carlo in *William Tell*. Three days ago, the proposal was more precise, and in the presence of several witnesses he repeated to me: "You must sing *William Tell* for us this summer. I'll take care of getting the royal authorization, and I guarantee you a tremendous success, profitable for us both."

Since the San Carlo is closed all next season, it is only in the exceptional case that he would open his big theater, and for solemn occasions. Everyone who heard this explicit proposal insisted on my accepting it, and here is what I replied:

"I don't say no, but leave me enough time to study the Italian language, the Italian accent."

"Eh! You speak Italian better than I," replied Barbaja. (He wasn't wrong about that, for the jargon that he speaks is of no country. It is a mixture of Milanese, French, and Neapolitan, in which there is very little good Italian.) And then he added: "I am not asking you to do this right away. But two months from now you must decide to make your debut in Naples with *William Tell*. I promise you a full house for twelve performances, and I'll give you a return on the receipts."

"Well, we'll talk about it some more," I answered. "I am going to continue working with Donizetti, whose advice has already done me so much good. And when I feel a little more Italian, when I have some chance of not offending your ears, which have good reason to be particular, I shall put myself at your disposal." We left each other with that.

The day before, I had met with Barbaja's son and one of his friends who is, I think, his intimate advisor. Both said to me: "Stay here instead of going to Milan. A success at the San Carlo is more widely known than successes anywhere else, and you will be able to find a good position for the autumn and carnival season. [If you go to Milan] we will be without a first tenor, while in Milan you will have a hard time working things out with Donzelli, who will want to sing the roles that suit you."

Donizetti had already indicated to me that he hoped the Milan business would not go through, and that he would like to see me work things out with Barbaja. I must say, however, that I suspect a debut with *William Tell* would not go down

well with him. Donizetti reigns supreme here, and he probably would not want to be compared with the high priest. But
he won't dare oppose it. Out of politics alone, he will do
everything to help my debut. Besides, *William Tell* is only
one opera, whereas the whole repertoire here belongs to him.
From another point of view, it is likely that *William Tell*, for
one reason or another, can have only a limited number of
performances here. I have told Donizetti about everything,
both the proposals of Barbaja and the letter from Rossini. By
turning down the Milan engagement I have given the appearance of following his advice.

That's how things stand now, and you can see that I have
more than one good reason to be consoled over the break with
Milan. I am more determined than ever not to leave Naples
before taking the big step. There is a marvelous opportunity
for me here. They have had no great talents for a long time.
[Giovanni] Bassadonna, their young tenor, sings pleasantly,
but he lacks resources and strength, and furthermore he is
going to the carnival. Everyone knows that I am working with
Donizetti, and that has a good effect. Donizetti already talks
about my progress, and his friends are already mine. By coming to study Italian singing in Naples I flatter the vanity and
the weakness of the public, who, in applauding me, will believe they are applauding one of their own children. It is in
Naples that I will have been trained. It is to the good taste of
the Neapolitans that I will owe my talent. I will be one of
them, and that is enough to assure my success. This, together

with all the reasons I have already given you, should suffice to make you want me to stay in Naples.[14]

Nourrit's letters to his wife at this time continue to dwell on the pros and cons of having her and others of the family, including the children, join him in Naples, the principal source of anxiety being the severity of the Neapolitan climate during the summer months. The letter of 4 April offers reassurances on this point, including medical opinion, then resumes under the date of 5 April:

Yesterday my cousin said good-bye and left for Rome. So now I am alone. Although I liked having him here, and shall probably feel a certain emptiness for a few days, I am far from regretting my loneliness. He caused me to waste a certain amount of time, and, further, I spoke French with him, and was often hesitant to do voice work for fear of bothering him. Now I can work without inhibition, and I assure you that with the way I am using my time the days go by quickly. Each hour has its purpose. In the evening, nevertheless, I feel that I could have done more during the day.

Here's how I am living. I get up early in the morning, between six and seven. I sing, I study Italian, I sing some more, and then I have breakfast. When the weather is good I go out for a moment before breakfast. After breakfast comes my Italian lesson, which lasts until eleven. When the teacher has left, I go to the post office. I return and read my mail when I have some, or write when I don't. I sing a little more, then go out to take my lesson with Donizetti.

For several days now we have changed our method of working. He is having me read new music, and I have to sing at sight with the right accent and musical dynamics. I have to pronounce and understand the words. This should help me to move along rapidly by giving me more assurance and accustoming my eyes and intelligence to quicker response. Then I take a long and beautiful walk. Here we have the most beautiful place in the world to walk, a superb garden along the seashore. They call it the Villa Reale. It is here that in summer all Naples comes to spend the evening and breathe the soft sea air by moonlight. After my walk I go home and study Italian for an hour and a half or two hours, and thus I come to show time. Although for the present the theater is not very interesting, I always go. It is an exercise for my ears which doesn't tire me too much.

There follows a paragraph italicized here to point out its significance for the future, the unwitting forecast of troubles to come:

You see, my dear, that my time is put to good use. I am still pleased with my work, and it seems to me that my voice has already improved, but I no longer know how to sing French. Recently I took to Donizetti some songs of Schubert's, and found myself rather embarrassed when I had to sing them for him. I could no longer find my French inflections, my usual effects, and I am not yet sufficiently familiar with my new manner to use it at once on music I have already sung. Entirely new Ital-

ian things are much better for my voice today than what I have sung a hundred times in France. . . . Good-bye, my dear. Thousands of kisses to be distributed among you all, and a thousand for you alone. Don't worry about me. I am pleased with my health and with my state of mind. Decidedly, this trip to Italy was an inspiration from heaven![15]

For the moment, certainly, Nourrit felt no anxiety about the transition from a French to an Italian method of vocal production, nor about the change from a French (Parisian) to an Italian cultural environment, as reflected in his letter to his wife of 10 April:

Have no fear, my dear, that the work to which I am devoting myself will make me lose any of my ideas for the future, my hopes for the application of art to a more elevated objective than most of our countrymen have in mind today. Quite the contrary. I feel that I am better situated to move faster toward the goal I am setting myself. Musical art in France doesn't extend beyond Paris, whereas Italian music is the music of all Europe, the music of the whole world. Furthermore, I shall be dealing with an unsophisticated public, a public that is not blasé, as ours is, toward all the artificial effects so lavishly presented in France. Heavens, what a lot of new things there are to be done here in Italy! I see already that Donizetti has confidence in my theatrical experience. If I stay here, as seems probable, the new works may well reflect my influence.

But, I repeat, I don't want to be in a hurry. I want to perfect myself so as to be sure of not failing at my first appearance. Donizetti is putting his weight behind getting me engaged here. He has already spoken to the superintendent of the theaters. You already know how Barbaja feels, and what he needs. He has no tenor for the autumn, and not a single one is available in Italy. Everyone here is counting on *William Tell*—if the police allow it. That's where I am headed. I work and work, come what may.

I haven't felt so at peace with myself for years. The future no longer worries me. I see my career opening up before me, and the difficulties I am encountering, far from disturbing me, give me more energy, more courage. It is a totally new career, and in order to start it confidently, I am not afraid of redoing my musical education. Finding myself back on the school benches even has a certain charm for me. It makes me feel twenty years younger. Donizetti takes more interest in me daily. He tries to find ways to make the work easier for me and to bring me along faster in securing an Italian accentuation. He has just put me on the vocal exercises of [Giulio] Bordogni.[16] You see, I am going back to the *ABC*s. Well, that truly pleases me. I feel as if I were being born again, to a new artistic life. I have discovered a new world, and each step brings me a new conquest, but at the same time reveals a new world to conquer. So, I am in no hurry to make my debut. I am convinced that the later I make it, the more outstanding it will be, since I will have more to bring to it.

You are probably surprised to hear me speak this way, and can't conceive of my having so much to do in order to succeed after all the success I have had. Try to understand, my dear, that it is a totally different system of producing the voice. Each day I notice all the harm the French language has done to my voice by making me pronounce it purely. There are, for example, two *a*s in French, the closed *a* as in *jamais* and the open *a* as in *théâtre*. The Italians have only one *a*, which is neither of ours. It alone is favorable for the production of the voice, whereas, of our two, one is too cramped and the other too free. That is what bothers me, that and our unfortunate nasal vowels, which do not exist in Italian, like *an*, *on*, and *in*, so many stiflers of resonance. When I appear at the San Carlo, I don't want people to say simply, "He sings Italian well for a Frenchman." My ambition is to have them say, "But one would think he was an Italian!"[17]

The following letter to his wife of 12 April gives the first intimation of a change of heart as to a debut with *William Tell*:

I must tell you that my enthusiasm about making my debut with *William Tell* has become somewhat dampened. I would just as soon begin with a role completely new to me, completely Italian, and less difficult than *Tell*, which I have sung in French. After an initial success in the Italian repertoire, Arnold would be good for a second decisive blow. But all that will be in the hands of God. I don't worry about it.[18]

A letter of 17 April, again to his wife, is devoted largely to continued speculation and uncertainty as to whether she should join him in Naples for the summer, and under what circumstances. But one paragraph gives a happy and optimistic account of a dinner party at Donizetti's where he sang for the composer and his guests:

He had me sing for them several passages from *Lucia*. I made a great impression, despite not being in the best of voice. . . . First, I had sung two songs by Schubert [presumably in French], which went well enough. But to tell the truth, my voice was completely different singing in Italian. I felt that I had ten times as much power in those cantilenas and with those words which are so sonorous. Everyone present already had a good opinion of me, both because of my reputation and because of what Donizetti had told them about me. But I seem to have surpassed their expectations. They were astonished both by my voice and by my accent, and especially by my powers of expression. They said that I had moved them as they hadn't been moved in years. Far from making me wish to hasten my debut, this first success only makes me more dedicated to my studies. If I have already made such progress in one month, what can I not expect from the future?[19]

On 29 April Nourrit could announce to his wife his engagement by Barbaja in a letter that also reflects his family's decision to join him in Naples:

There is no turning back now, my dear. I am now Italian, at least for the next eleven months. I signed my agreement with Barbaja yesterday. The financial conditions are not as good as those offered me in Milan, but the position is a hundred times better, and the chance of success much greater, since I shall be making my debut in an opera by Donizetti written expressly for me, and of which I have chosen the subject. It is the one I dreamed about when I left France, the *Polyeucte* of Corneille, in which I have found some fine musical situations. You know what confidence I shall have in the feelings I must express in this role of a Christian martyr. You will share this confidence, and we shall both be reassured by the knowledge that it is not just personal interest that makes us want success. The hope of contributing to a true work of art will support me more than a vain desire for glory. With this work, I hope to embark upon an altogether new career, a career such as I have always wished for. The subject is all the more pleasing to Donizetti because it is absolutely new to Italy. It gives him the possibility of doing something different from what he has done until now. He is becoming quite excited about the Christians, and is counting on the effect of the religious chants in the midst of dramatic situations.

First your father, then my mother, and now you express pleasure that the Milan business didn't work out, and you urge me to accept Barbaja's offers. You have already understood from my last letter to Eugène [her brother] that I was afraid you would regret my not making my debut in *William*

Tell, and now I see that you have anticipated the very objections that persuaded me to give it up. Finally, you seem to be reassured about the stay in Naples as far as the children are concerned, and I will look forward to embracing you a month from now, a month and a few days.

You can imagine the pleasure with which I signed my engagement with Barbaja. If your father and my mother think I was a bit undemanding about the financial conditions, I hope they will nonetheless be satisfied with the good position I shall have in thus beginning, and that they will think it worth the sacrifice on my part. In the last analysis, there is nothing degrading about the engagement. I am to make my debut in September or October at the latest with the performance of a new opera, and I am to remain until 20 March or Easter, as I wish. They give me 600 ducats a month, or 2,700 francs, plus one-half a performance at the San Carlo not in the subscription series. That could bring in an additional 3,000 or 4,000 francs, perhaps more if I make a complete success of it and can make it lively. That is enough to cover our expenses for the year.

Barbaja is beaming about my engagement, and has already sent to the printers his *cartello* with my name on it in big letters. He is a strange man, very amusing, very gruff and basically not too tightfisted for an Italian impresario.[20]

A letter of 6 May tells of Nourrit's having found a suitable dwelling for his family, due to arrive in only a few weeks:

For my part, I have been trying to find you a pleasant lodging, and I think I have succeeded. The location is delightful. Your windows will look out on the promenade. I told you about the Villa Reale. Our children will have only to cross the street to be under the trees bordering the seashore. Under their shade, even in the midst of summer, it is always cool.

Meanwhile, our *Polyeucte* is coming along. The librettist is at work, and Donizetti is already worrying about what he must do to enter into the character of this Christian music, a subject new to him. I am not sorry to see him having a few doubts about himself. That is a good thing for those who have too great a facility. I have more and more confidence in this theme, and I hope that you share that confidence.[21]

Two days later, obviously already concerned with the effect his new style of singing might have on those who had known him only as the greatest *French* tenor of his time, he wrote:

Don't think, my dear, that the work I am doing is changing me to the point that you will no longer be able to hear me as sympathetically as you used to. This is entirely a technical matter. It is the *quality* of my voice that I seek to improve. When you used to take pleasure in hearing me, it was not the beauty of my voice that affected you. . . . The change you will find in me will be barely perceptible. If you don't understand clearly all the words that come out of my mouth, you will nevertheless share the emotion that I have to impart. For the heart, there is only one language, only one accent, so you may rest assured that for you nothing of me will be lost. Furthermore, I repeat, this progress, which Donizetti sees, this change which he points out, is largely for the Italian ear. For you, it will not amount to anything. So, be calm. Whether or not my voice is changing, my musical feeling is always the same. What you used to appreciate in my talent you will still find there. You had better prepare the family to see me with a mustache.[22]

Madame Nourrit, accompanied by her brother, arrived in Naples on 10 June and, with the children, moved into the quarters arranged for them by Nourrit in the Villa Barbaja, a floor above that occupied by Barbaja himself. Her brother returned almost immediately to Paris. A letter she wrote to him on 26 June makes it clear that the tenor's misgivings about how she might react to the changes in his vocalism were all too well founded.

I would like to say one word about Adolphe. You ask what impression I was left with after the audition at Donizetti's. A good one. But I can't say the same for the exercises I hear them putting him through. All that I can say for my own reassurance is that I don't understand them. This voice, which was so pure and varied in its inflections, is no longer the same. In volume it is beautiful and ringing. But aside from volume, it is weak and broken. The impression I have is such that I close all the doors so that I won't hear. And I must hide this impression, for I am fully convinced that I cannot judge the work Adolphe is doing, nor what he should do in order to sing in the Italian manner.

I am a good judge of music, of singing, perhaps, with respect to the final result. But I know nothing of the mechanics, least of all those of Italian singing. You know, in these times, I don't attach much importance to Italian art. I had thought that Adolphe should bring his talents to Italy, thinking they would be great enough to make people overlook his failings. But I had not understood that he was completely to transform himself. . . . It is not that I think Adolphe has no progress to make, but I think it is not here that he will make it. I could be mistaken, of course, and, in any case, there is no turning back. Adolphe must find success here, or he must stop singing. He thinks he is on the right path to success. He is a better judge of the matter than I. What I might say would only cause him worry and discouragement. So I shall remain silent. Besides, the damage is done, if damage there be. These are sad words, Eugène. But I feel that I owe you the whole truth. I will return to this subject, but you are the only person with whom I shall discuss it.[23]

What she wrote must, upon reflection, have frightened even her, for three days later, on 29 June, she wrote to her brother again in a more cheerful vein. Obviously she was making every effort to come to terms with a situation she could, in any case, do nothing about, and trying to see things in a brighter light. Her low opinion of Italian art cannot have helped.

The fears I expressed to you are not based on any uncertainty as to Adolphe's success here. I am counting on that. I fear only that it may be bought at too high a price, and at the expense of qualities not much valued here, but which I believe to be superior to those one finds in Italy. You, who have a higher opinion than I of Italian art, probably won't be concerned about what I think. You might, at the very most, be concerned about seeing me unhappy and sad. Don't worry. I am less so than when I wrote you on Tuesday. Despite my resolve not to let Adolphe have any notion of what I was thinking, my worry and agitation were such that in the end I had to tell him at least a part of what was on my mind. I am glad that I did. It doesn't seem to have bothered him, and I feel a little more at peace with myself. It is not that I am absolutely satisfied with the reasons he gives me as the motives for his new work. I just feel that I must accept them. And this I do.

I finally did find one reason, a small one, that nevertheless gives me some consolation. I said to myself that Adolphe has a new role to play, that of an Italian singer, and that, just as he changed his voice and his demeanor in order to play the part of an old Jew [Éléazar], or a peasant [Masaniello], or a young knight [Raoul], he changes them today in order to sing in the Italian manner. I think that is what he finds so fascinating. Certainly, after he had studied Robert [le diable] for six months, and after he had sung it for six more months, his voice no longer had its freshness and timbre. The same thing is happening now. But even if his voice is changing, his intelligence is growing, and I say again: It gives me some consolation to think so. I wanted to tell you of this comforting change that has come into my thoughts so as not to leave you too long with the bad impression my last letter must have left.[24]

If Nourrit had been disturbed or nettled by his wife's observations, he revealed no discomfiture in his letters to his family and others over the next few weeks. They are uniformly cheerful and optimistic, reporting splendid progress with *Poliuto* (which he always refers to as *Polyeucte*), although confiding, in a letter of 6 July to Hiller in Bellagio, some apprehension about the possible reaction of the censors to the opera's subject matter. Nourrit expresses willingness to have his hero be something less than a saint, but not to having him be anything other than a Christian.[25]

To his brother-in-law he wrote on 26 July:

As to my studies, I pursue them with more ardor than ever. It seems to me that since Adèle is with me, my work is more methodical and more relaxed. Each week I am able to note progress. If I try to do too much, Adèle is there to counsel moderation. It seems to me that I am less preoccupied with my pronunciation, with my Italian accent, and Donizetti corrects me only at long intervals. Another few months, and Italian will be my mother tongue.[26]

The blow fell on 12 August, when *Poliuto* was formally prohibited by the censors. But Nourrit did not quite give up all hope. To his brother-in-law he wrote on 16 August:

I regret, dear brother, that you have learned of the difficulties we have encountered with the subject of *Polyeucte*. I had hoped it would not be mentioned to you until all was irrevocably settled. The king [Ferdinand II] does not wish the Christian religion to be presented on the stage, either in good light or in bad. It reminds me of all that Manuel [García] told you in Genoa, and my experience has proved him an all too good judge of Italy. No need to tell you all that the prohibition of our *Polyeucte* has given me to think about. . . .

It is now up to me to attain very, very quickly some little reputation in this country and then return to France, and just at the moment when one would wish to escape from the mess into which the theater art there tumbles more disastrously every day. Sometime, when I am less pressed, we can discuss all that at our leisure. While awaiting [the decision], we changed the characters, the setting, and even the religion of our Christian martyr. We made him a fire-eater without changing either the dramatic situations or the sentiments. May God will it that this transmutation will satisfy the royal censor. The work will suffer, no doubt, but I hope that if it is thus adapted, the public will be unwilling to see anything there but Christians.[27]

Any hope of salvaging *Poliuto* was vain, and on 4 September Nourrit wrote to Mme Aucoc, his sister:

It has not been God's wish that I make my Italian debut with *Poliuto* [his first use of the Italian title]. Despite all the hopes

I had pinned on that work, not just for playing my part, but for rejoicing in doing so, I shall doubtless find in my submission the strength I had hoped to find in the expression of feelings congenial to me. Italy is, perhaps, not disposed to accept profound and elevated emotions. The theater here is nothing but a distraction. It has little time for anything of a serious nature. And then the church here is at a point where it was with us under the Restoration. By way of opposition to a power far too domineering, the public rejects everything that might have a religious character. Thus, in playing Polyeucte, I would actually have had a battle on my hands. Not that it frightened me. I hoped to emerge with glory. No doubt I deceived myself, since that battle has been denied me.

For the rest, I am content with the role that is to serve for my debut [Donizetti's *Pia de' Tolomei*, first given in Venice on 18 February 1837], and as an actor I shall have far more to do than in *Polyeucte*.

And then, all these prohibitions of the revised version have visibly offended the public, who have sided with the theater and, above all, with me. It seems that everyone is now interested in me, and that my success will be that much more certain the more difficult it becomes.[28]

In the event, Nourrit was not content with *Pia de' Tolomei*, and told his brother-in-law as much in a letter of 22 September. Indeed, he did not sing it, not because of dissatisfaction with the role, but because his voice failed him at rehearsal, and he had to withdraw, as he explained sadly in a letter to Eugène dated 13 October:

What all has passed through my poor head since I last wrote to you! How many changes of ideas, and what struggles with myself. The last fortnight has been the most painful of my life, and if the good that I may draw from this test is in proportion to the bad, I can await the future with confidence. Adèle has already told you rather more about me than we wanted my mother and your father to know. But since I don't know to what extent she has told you the whole truth, I shall talk to you as if you knew nothing.

The rejection of *Polyeucte* was a terrible blow, as I had so counted on it for the impression it would make upon an Italian public that in my head I built an entire future on the success of that debut. Things have now taken such a turn that I am inclined to reckon it a favor that the king prevented it. In order to make all that clear to you, I must take up the tale from some distance back.

You and Adèle, when you heard me here, were surprised at the change that had taken place in my singing, the surprise not unmixed with a bit of regret. You both observed that in gaining certain qualities (or at least in developing them), I had lost others equally essential. Despite the satisfaction that I displayed, I fully shared your regret, and hoped always that with time I could recover those fine nuances that were the essence of my talent, and the variety of inflection I had had to abandon in order to conform to the exigencies of Italian singing as one hears it today, and as it is effective in Italy.

In my role of Polyeucte, I did indeed encounter certain

difficulties that prompted me to this new manner of producing the tone always at full strength. But since almost the entire role was one of exaltation, I was sustained by what I was expressing, and the emotion of my delivery covered the faults of my voice, which was called upon to do no more than express lugubrious or energetic sentiments, and had become incapable of rendering the tender or melancholy inflections that had always been native to me. You both saw me so full of confidence in my work that you hesitated to trouble me with your observations.

Adèle, without telling me, hoped, as I did, that with time I would be able to unite my old qualities with the new. And I, confident to the point of blindness, to the point of forgetting myself in all that Donizetti told me, believed that the size of the San Carlo would obscure certain faults that shocked me in a room. There my fault, there my error!

Futile to recall all that persuaded me to accept the role in *Pia* after having refused it for a full month. Partly out of consideration for Donizetti, partly to spare the management embarrassment, I had the weakness to take on an ineffective role in a mediocre opera. Ah, well, despite all the discomfiture it gave me, I should once more reckon it a blessing, since I can thank that bad role in that mediocre opera for having opened my eyes to the error of my ways. With nothing to express but sentiments that are most ordinary, or rather lowly and odious, I found myself face to face with the new accents I had acquired. Their falseness and exaggeration struck me the first time I heard them resound in the San Carlo. They made me ashamed of myself, and then I lost my head. As a consequence of my stay in Naples, my old voice was no longer at my disposal, and with my new studies my mixed voice and head voice had vanished. I was so displeased with my artificial accents that I determined to make no use of them.

So, I believed the future lost, at least for the theater. I thought of the mischief that six months of forced study had done to me, six months of following a wrong path. I thought I could never rediscover my natural voice, that voice whose use had been so inhibited for seven months that I found it impossible to rediscover the slightest inflection. You can imagine my despair. My acceptance of the role in *Pia* made the termination of my engagement the more difficult. It would involve an expensive law suit that I stood a good chance of losing, for hardly any Italian would understand why I should insist on making a debut in one role rather than another. For them a role is a pretext for offering a couple of arias, a duet, a trio, a finale—and that's that.

What troubled me was to see that Barbaja was still counting on me while I, for my part, had no hope of singing again, or at least believed that it would take as much time to repair the damage as it had taken to do it. Despite his abrupt manner, I have appreciated Barbaja under these circumstances. He has understood my position, and has sympathized sincerely. He has spared me the embarrassment of a tedious law suit that in behalf of his associates, he could not have avoided, and has given me the time necessary to get myself into shape, saying to me: "You will not sing until you tell me you are ready to do so. If, in fact, you cannot, then your presence here during the term of your engagement will protect you from any chicanery on the part of my associates, who will have nothing to claim from you as long as they have paid you nothing."

My role was given to Bassadonna. *Pia* was performed without success, and everyone in Naples believed that I feigned indisposition in order to spare myself embarrassment and not offend Donizetti.

Since then I have been resting, that is, singing not at all, or almost not at all, for my head hardly rests. I should say, however, that my French voice is almost completely back, although I must treat it carefully in order to restore its former flexibility and accustom it to hard work and fatigue.

Barbaja has asked the minister of police, who has accompanied the king to Sicily, to authorize a production of *William Tell*, and as soon as I feel fit to sing, I shall introduce myself to the Neapolitan public with my French accents, with that voice that so pleased Rossini and moved the Milanese public, without troubling myself about a more or less open *a*, about a nasal sound, or a throaty inflection.

Delacroix, the painter, was right when he said that an artist is not truly worth anything until he has resigned himself to his shortcomings. That is what I did in France, and it is what I must now do in Italy. Good God! I am French. What is so bad if they say that I have a French accent just as long as I sing well? To tell the truth, with the Italian inflection that I have cultivated, I have only one color at my disposal, and I find myself falling into precisely those errors for which we reproach the Italians. I have sinned through an excess of humility. I denied my gods, and I am punished.

You will now understand that all my dreams about Italy have evaporated. If I have a future, it is no longer here. With Donizetti's departure [he had left Naples for Paris] and the stupidities of the censor, there is nothing left for me in this country but to introduce myself as advantageously as possible, to stick with *William Tell*, and, if that is denied me, to put the French press to work protesting against the persecution that will oblige me to accept a role in which I cannot be seen and heard to advantage.

I should, however, tell you that if *William Tell* is denied me, then Barbaja is offering me a role which appeals to me greatly in a score new to Naples and which has had a great success in all Italy. It is Mercadante's *Il giuramento*.[29] It is a beautiful score, rather in the style of the German school, a score that pleases me and suits me, including a lovely duet that should create a great sensation. This work breaks with all that has been heard in Naples, and may be of a kind to modify Neapolitan taste. But I shall not accept it until *Tell* has been turned down, and until I have sung it to myself as I think it should be sung and am satisfied with myself.

And there, dear Eugène, is where I am. To tell you the whole truth, I must add that this state of uncertainty sits badly with me. I am impatient, and although I know that my voice needs to be treated most gently if it is to recover, I test it too often and tire it more than I should. Then come the dissatisfactions, the discouragements, and the most deplorable weaknesses. You will understand that the hard lesson I have just received has inevitably affected my spirits, and I am beset by lamentable misgivings and ever-recurring uncertainties.

That is what I am working to conquer at the moment. It is essential that I regain complete confidence in myself. Your good sister helps me as best she can. It is she who sustains me, who gives me courage. Indeed, I don't know what would have become of me had I not had her by my side. Thank God that she preserves her health amidst these adversities and that the children enjoy a well-being such as they have not experienced since coming to Naples. Don't mention this letter to my mother. If she knew that you had received it, she would want to read it.[30]

This letter was not posted immediately, and two days later, on 15 October, Nourrit added a less gloomy postscript:

I closed my letter the day before yesterday still sad, uncertain, and dissatisfied with myself. Now today, with my disposition utterly changed, I do not wish to let that letter leave without telling you that I am entirely content with my voice, that I have it as I want it, that I find it even better than before.

If that continues to be the case, it is I who will be nagging Barbaja to let me sing. I have just had another look at the role in *Il giuramento*. It suits me perfectly. There is a duet which in Naples should be a counterpart to the duet in *Les Huguenots*. So, I await impatiently the minister's verdict on *William Tell*. If it is delayed too long, I may take it upon myself to make a debut as soon as possible with *Il giuramento*.

For me, uncertainty is the worst of evils. It was that which blinded me to the point of accepting *Pia* for a debut. But as today I have some elbow room, if I take *Il giuramento*, it is the work and the role that persuade me (as the Italians say). I am satisfied that I shall be doing something worthy of an artist in applying all my interpretive faculties to the performance of this work which, I repeat, is of a genre entirely new to Naples, and in which there is plenty of substance to create a small revolution in public taste. Also, while always looking out for my voice, I wish to devote myself exclusively to this role, and make as much of it as possible.[31]

A day later, in a second postscript, Nourrit wrote:

Bad weather prevented the departure of this letter, and Adèle wishes me to tell you how things stand with me as of today. My poor head is like the sky above Naples in the bad season: plenty of clouds, wind, rain, and a few rays of sunshine—but of a brilliant sun. The fact is that I have been unable to enjoy two days of calm, two days of satisfaction. It is the most I can hope for if a day comes to an end as it began.

In the morning I am convinced that it is only my head that is ailing, and that my voice is in perfect shape. A few hours later I go to the piano, and it's the other way around. It is my voice that is ailing, and all my anxieties are justified.

I would have wished to spare you the catalogue of my worries, my doubts, my trouble. But your sister obliged me to tell you the whole truth, and open myself to you without reservation. The truth is that head and voice are both in a bad state. Is it that one affects the other? That is the question. But in any case, we find ourselves in a vicious circle from which we know not how to escape. Patience, patience—and more patience! Then, afterwards, we have to say: courage! More likely: resignation![32]

How his wife viewed Nourrit's situation and condition at that time is set forth in a letter she wrote to her brother, dated 20 October:

Nothing new except that Adolphe has appeared to be in good health for four days, and that his voice is improving. He has given up the *voix sombrée*, which he had tried to develop, and is now trying to go back to where he was when he arrived in Naples. I regret having to say this, but it is the truth. Do you remember one day in Paris when, after reading a letter from Adolphe in which he spoke of his new studies, I said I was sorry to see him begin again like that? You were surprised at my reaction. But it was well founded as you can see. No, Adolphe should not have come to Italy to change his art. At his age it was madness. If he could not be accepted just as he was, or by altering his style a little, he should not even have tried. (You saw my impression of this change in the first letter I wrote to you in Rome.) But he went much farther than I had imagined. It is his voice he tried to change! And in spite of my wish to hide my feelings from relatives and friends, I fear that it showed through in my letters as well as in my conversation with Adolphe. I have not changed my mind.

I did see a means of having some success in that way of singing if well applied in *Polyeucte*, and I accepted it, thinking the damage was done and there was no remedy for it. My fear may have been excessive. By returning to his natural voice, Adolphe has regained some of the qualities he had before, and it is possible that time will restore the greater part. It cannot be said, however, that he has the finesse and charm that he had. Besides, age would probably have taken away these qualities, and they had already begun to diminish. They will be replaced by greater evenness in tone and more energy.[33]

Plate 1

Adolphe Nourrit, the first great dramatic tenor.
Engraving by Delarue after a drawing by Bourdet.

Plate 2

Giovanni-Battista Rubini,
1794–1854, an Italian
tenor eight years Nourrit's
senior. Engraving by
Lemercier after an
original by Deveria.

Plate 3

Gilbert-Louis Duprez,
1806–1896, the French
tenor whose engagement by
the Paris Opéra following
his success in Italy
prompted Nourrit to
leave the Opéra and seek
a new career in Italy.

Manuel García, Sr.,
1775–1832, Rossini's first
Almaviva in *Il barbiere
di Siviglia* and Nourrit's
vocal teacher. Also among
his pupils were his
children, Maria Malibran,
Pauline Viardot, and
Manuel García, Jr.

Manuel García, Jr.,
1805–1906, like his father
a vocal teacher, and a
friend and contemporary of
Nourrit's. Oil painting by
John Singer Sargent.

Plate 6

Nourrit as Masaniello in Auber's *La muette de Portici*.

Plate 7

As Robert in Meyerbeer's *Robert le diable*.

Plate 8

As Éléazar in Halévy's *La Juive*.

Plate 9

As Raoul in Meyerbeer's *Les Huguenots.*

Plate 10

As Orphée in Gluck's opera of the same name.

Plate 11

As Gustave in Auber's *Gustave III ou
Le bal masqué.*

Plate 12

As Don Juan in Mozart's *Don Giovanni*.

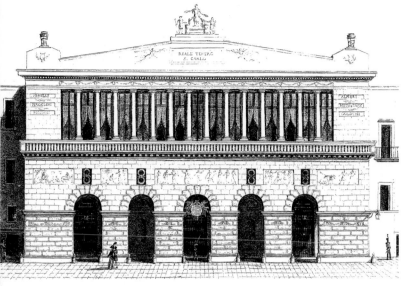

Plate 13

The Teatro San Carlo in Naples, as it appeared in
Nourrit's time and, indeed, as it appears today.
Watercolor drawing.

Plate 14

The interior of the San Carlo in Naples, much as it
appeared in Nourrit's time. The performance in progress
(obviously nearing its conclusion) is of the opera *L'ultimo
giorno di Pompei* by Giovanni Pacini (1796–1867), first
given at the San Carlo on 19 November 1825 and an
enormous success at the time. Watercolor drawing.

Part 4

ITALY: The Artist (Success, Failure, Success,
Disappointment, Despair, Disaster)

Nourrit's four days of good health and improved vocal condition prompted this letter to his brother-in-law dated 25 October:

My last letter must certainly have upset you, as I confided to you all my misgivings, vicissitudes, doubts, and terrors, and you will be glad to learn that I have finally emerged from the miserable state in which I have been for the past month. It was all in my head, and uncertainty was at the root of it. I have now cut that root by putting an end to uncertainty. Having received no response in the matter of *William Tell*, I have boldly decided to accept *Il giuramento*, and this time I believe I have made a good choice. I have had plenty of time to study my role, to evaluate its potential, to appreciate its beauties. Adèle is at least as satisfied as I with this score, which is truly beautiful, and capable of bringing about a change in Neapolitan taste. The work is eagerly awaited— has indeed been anticipated for a long time—and everything points to a premiere under the most favorable auspices. My prima donna is to be Mme [Adelina Salvi-] Spech,[1] a young and pretty person whose talent is praised, especially as an actress. With her, something fine can be made of the last act, which is of a kind to move deeply a public not overly exposed to tragic effects.

My role is well in my voice, and yesterday evening I astonished some Italian friends by singing some passages from the last act. In the morning I had sung for a French artist who was stupefied by the progress my voice has made. I can tell you today that I am utterly content with it, and that I don't even regret the intensive study with Donizetti. I owe to him a superior sound and more breadth of phrase. Now that I have rediscovered my head voice and my natural timbre, I wish for nothing more than to maintain myself in this estate. I content myself for the moment with what I have, without wishing to acquire anything more. I count on handling myself in the rehearsals in such a way as to have all my resources fresh and well reposed, come the day of the great challenge.

Please reassure your father about the effect of my withdrawal from *Pia*. Far from putting me in the wrong, it has given me among the Neapolitan public and my fellow artists the reputation of a man of spirit and good sense. No one believes in my indisposition. They see in my conduct nothing but an honorable maneuver to extricate myself from a bad role without offending Donizetti. I need not tell you that Donizetti made nothing of my withdrawal, and I can assure you that since that moment he has redoubled his display of affection and devotion. You have doubtless seen him, and you may be certain that we parted the best of friends.[2]

Nourrit's spirits remained buoyant with the commencement of rehearsals for *Il giuramento*, and in a letter to his mother in early November he could tell her:

We have begun rehearsals for *Il giuramento*, and each day I am more and more content with what I have done. It is a lovely work, eagerly awaited in Naples, and my role offers at least two good scenes where I appear to best advantage. I have already tried one or two effects that have had a great impact upon my colleagues. I have nothing but praise for my environment. I have already told you how satisfied I have been with Barbaja's conduct toward me. I find among my colleagues the most cordial good will, and that gives me confidence in myself. Those who heard me at the rehearsals of *Pia* don't recognize me. It is another voice, another talent, another artist that they discover in me, and they all applaud me enthusiastically for not having made my debut in that bad role which I had had the weakness to accept. I am of good hope, for it is now with confidence that I launch myself, and the public is well disposed toward me. I hope that you will have seen M. Édouard Bertin,[3] who heard me the day of his departure, and that you will know of the impression I made upon him.

Whatever troubles I may have had, I can only congratulate myself on all that I have done and all that has happened to me. In fact, I have gained in talent, and my resources have been enriched in a manner that would have been out of the question had I remained in France doing nothing but what I had always done. A bit of courage still, a bit more patience, and we shall again thank Providence which has led everything toward the best possible end.[4]

He wrote in a similar vein to his brother-in-law by the same post, adding, with respect to his wife:

Adèle also is calm. She is content with my role and the way I project it. Poor Adèle! I owe it to her to succeed, if only to reward her for all the trouble my frailty has caused her. . . . It is thanks to her that I have not succumbed to my agitation. Without her it is certain that I could have been capable of foolishness. But, thank God, the storm has passed, and we sail with a favorable wind. A few days from now I shall be able to reckon by the way the rehearsals go, how much time we shall need to give to *Il giuramento*. The music is more difficult than that which is played here every day.[5]

The premiere took place on 14 November, and Nourrit had a brilliant success, as recounted in a letter of 22 November to his brother-in-law:

You who have known all my sufferings, all my battles, all my frailties, you whom I have called to bear witness to the violent struggles I have had to endure, you should hear from me now of all my raptures. It behooves me to tell you, without reserve, without modesty, all about my triumph, and to tell it to you as if it were not I who was the victor.

Since the day that Bertin heard me, I regained courage and self-confidence, my voice regaining little by little its former flexibility while losing nothing of what I had gained through my studies with Donizetti. I recovered gradually all my former attributes. I was, however, not completely master of my effects until we began the rehearsals of *Il giuramento*. But the progress I made each day led me to hope that I could finally reach the goal I had set myself: to unite charm and strength, expressiveness and clarity. At the rehearsals, my colleagues did everything possible to encourage me. They had felt sympathy for me when they saw the condition I was in during the rehearsals of *Pia*, and each of them seemed disposed to give me a slap on the shoulder to guarantee against a relapse from which I might not manage to recover. But then I already sensed in myself the strength to go forward and even to struggle against the obstacles.

The role in *Il giuramento* appealed to me. I was convinced of the work's worth. It was written in the French style (it is a fusion of Italian melody, German harmony, and French declamation). I had one scene which alone, perhaps, could make a good role. And then, I had regained my natural expressive resources. I was singing not just with my throat, but with my soul. I had become myself again. And as I had experienced all the phases of fear, I was on familiar terms with strong emotions. Those slight palpitations of the heart that I sometimes felt while tackling a new passage in front of my colleagues troubled me no longer.

The more we proceeded through the rehearsals, the more my role gained in importance, and those who had heard me in *Pia* no longer recognized me. At last, the first time I sang seriously the final duet, which is very tragic, I saw faces pale and eyes fill with tears. [Giuseppe] Festa,[6] the conductor, was overcome with emotion at the end, and I was showered with compliments from everyone. The husband of the prima donna, [Lorenzo] Salvi, who had just sung the role in Genoa and Brescia, had the courtesy to tell me that neither he nor any other of the tenors who have sung Viscardo drew so much from that scene.

Despite all this encouragement, I had one last test to face, and this was dangerous. I had been so displeased with my voice when I heard it in the San Carlo during the rehearsal of *Pia* that I entered that vast vault with foreboding. I had tried my voice in the theater that morning, but without accompaniment I could not gauge exactly the effect of the sonority in that auditorium, the largest in the world. Thus, I was very nervous at the first general rehearsal, and I was unhappy with the first sounds I uttered. This put me off a bit, but I didn't let it discourage me, and I continued without undue worry.

Although not quite content with this first tryout, I nevertheless looked forward to a second with confidence. After the second, which went better than the first, I counted on a third to give me a good idea of the quantity and quality of sound that would be required in that enormous auditorium. This preoccupation did not prevent me from giving myself over entirely to the expression of the music I had to sing, and the applause of my colleagues grew ever more enthusiastic, so much so that at the last rehearsal the effect I produced was very great, and was appreciated by all. Word spread about town, and the public was already so predisposed in my favor that if, at the premiere, I had not lived up to expectations, this would have been put down to nerves. In Naples, the judgment of the orchestra has a powerful influence on public opinion.

These rehearsals continued day after day in such a way that, while studying the effect of my voice, I also had to measure my resources. A year has passed since I last sang in a theater, and one cannot take things easily in Italy as one can in France. Even if you have a bit of fever, you sing. And then, operas are staged in twenty days. After three general rehearsals, you are onstage. So, I also had this to worry about, and always rehearsing seriously, I had to take care to be in good voice for the premiere.

Come the great day, and from early morning I felt my voice to be in better shape than it had been for a long time. I passed the day in a state of extraordinary tranquility. Never, even in Paris, have I been so relaxed on the day of a premiere. By an incredible bit of good fortune, certain shadings which I had thus far been unable to rediscover were suddenly there the moment I stepped on the stage. Despite excitement so violent that my legs were shaking, I sang my first number, a delicate, touching romance, as I had never managed to sing it before, during the rehearsals or even at home. At the last notes, the whole house came down. My success in Naples was secure, for they had already recognized in me a good vocal style, pure and Italian.

Now I have nothing to tell you of the effect of that performance. I'll let the critics do the talking. Their words are glorious. . . . You will see from what I have said about Mercadante's score how Italian taste is veering toward dramatic music, and although in Naples one pronounces *musica francese* with a horrible grimace, you will see that it is our school that is invading Italy.

I don't, however, see how much progress can be made against the rigors of censorship here. To make dramatic music you must have drama, and it is impossible to make drama under the prevailing conditions. I doubt, moreover, that my stay in Italy will be of long duration, and, thank God, I am now in a position to choose the gate through which it will suit me to reenter Paris. I have nothing specific in mind. I wait, confident of the future.

My return to the Opéra is, perhaps, no longer possible. But it is essential that the government sees fit to reorganize that institution, which has experienced deterioration and demolition in the hands of Duponchel. Otherwise, its commercial underpinnings may collapse if given a bit more time. True, the government has other fish to fry. But I can think of returning to Paris only to devote myself to art, to found or reestablish some theatrical institution from which artists may profit. Let's hope that such an opportunity may arise!

I have just enjoyed another success that will give you no less pleasure than that of the San Carlo. I went yesterday to thank Crescentini for a courtesy visit the grand old man had graciously paid me (he lives at the Conservatory). While I was descending the steps to his lodging, two or three students came up to me to compliment me, and invited me to see the canteen, where some 150 to 200 of their fellow students were assembled. As soon as they saw me enter, they all rose to their feet and applauded me so enthusiastically that I was utterly overcome, and had to withdraw with tears in my eyes.

I have been well rewarded for all my vicissitudes and tribulations. Whatever future is left for me, I must applaud my grand decision, and I don't think I have paid too much for my success in Naples. Now I must sustain it, and that is what I am working at. At the moment I am studying [Rossini's] *Otello* in order to be ready when the time comes. They want to mount another opera [*Elena da Feltre*] of Mercadante's immediately, which he wrote expressly for Naples, but which had to be delayed last year because of illness. One even speaks of *Don Giovanni* [with Nourrit as the Don]! What a triumph for me if I could put *Don Giovanni* over in Naples! As for *William Tell*, no need to count upon it.

When you see Donizetti, please give him my compliments. He thinks he may be able to put on *Polyeucte* at the Opéra in an adaptation by Scribe. The work, as it stands, is not suited to the Opéra. I think the maestro would do well to wait for me. What do you say?[7]

Further details of Nourrit's success in *Il giuramento* and of his plans for the immediate and not so immediate future went off to Paris in a letter to his father-in-law dated 23 November:

Yesterday, for the fifth time, I appeared before the public at the San Carlo, and always with the same welcome. Barbaja, yesterday, sent off a glowing account to Rossini, telling him that never in Naples had he made so much money from four performances of a new work as from *Il giuramento*. He begs me to stay with him all next year, and is ready to pay what I ask. But I am making no decision for the moment. First, I feel that I must appear in at least three roles to determine how secure I am in the favor of the public, and also to determine whether or not the role of Italian singer is entirely congenial to me. One must work here quite differently than in France. Here they have given me a new role in an opera by Mercadante that goes into rehearsal in two days. And then I most hold myself in readiness for *Otello*. Beyond that, I shall probably soon be obliged to sing either *Roberto*[8] or *Pia* to keep the repertoire going, the latter just once when the tenor, Bassadonna, is away. The censorship makes things very difficult for poor Barbaja. What he has decided upon one day he has to abandon the next. That is not conducive to persuading me to remain long in this country.

Then, I wish to know what is going on in Paris, and the effect of the news of my success, before signing anything for Italy. Thank God, I am now in a position to pick and choose, and I want to take advantage of it. You, dear father, give me your advice. As much as I would like to return to France, to see you all again, to embrace my mother, if it is your judgment that for my talent, and in the interests of the future, I should remain for some time in Italy, I am prepared to submit to the tedium and exactions of the Italian theaters. I have already gone too far to stop halfway, especially since the going is now easier. . . . I continue to be pleased with my voice, and compatriots who hear me compliment me on my progress and loss of weight.[9]

Nourrit was deceiving himself about the going becoming easier, or rather, at the time of writing, the truth had not dawned. In the event, his success had not made things easier for him. It made them more difficult. He had succeeded in a work unique of its kind in Italy, better suited to his talent and disposition than any other work in the repertoire of the Italian houses. He could not go on forever singing *Il giuramento*, yet no similarly congenial work was in prospect. As a result of his success—and subsequent personal successes in Mercadante's unsuccessful *Elena da Feltre* and Bellini's *Norma*—he was in demand all over Italy, but every offer of an engagement was coupled with conditions he found unacceptable. He wanted assurances of an important premiere, preferably in an opera written for him and tailored to his vocal and dramatic assets and inclinations, but no theater was prepared to give that assurance. All the houses required of their artists that they commit themselves to four performances a week, but Nourrit would agree to only three. The Italian custom of scheduling rehearsals every morning, and both morning and evening on days when there was no performance, appalled him, and the helter-skelter organization of

repertoire was a horror to one accustomed to the more orderly management of affairs at an institution such as the
Opéra. All this is spelled out in a letter Nourrit wrote, probably in January 1839, to a French bass, Gustave Euzet,[10]
who had sought his counsel about the advisability of coming
to Italy.

I am especially proud of having succeeded in Italy since
French artists see fit to rejoice in my success. For us, it is a
matter of nationality, of patriotism. Thank you, my dear com-
rades! I am always one of you, and though I have borrowed
the sonorous accents of the Italian language, it has been with
my French attributes that I have presented myself at the San
Carlo. You may rest assured of that. It is, perhaps, precisely
because of my qualities as a French artist that I have earned
the applause of the Italian public.

You know that I have not arrived at this happy denouement without distress. Only after eight months of work, tedium, difficulties, and setbacks was I finally permitted to
present myself in a congenial role and bring to a happy end-
ing the rather mad project upon which I had embarked. I call
my project, my enterprise, mad because, now that it has
ended, and ended well, I review what I have done and am
stunned by my lack of judgment, my lack of prudence. I
risked losing in one evening the fruit of sixteen years of work;
the successes of my whole career could have been wiped out
in that one evening. Truth to tell, in all that I did, I have been
more fortunate than wise, and I am moved today to indulge in

these reflections by the importance of the advice you seek of me.

Italy, my dear friend, is more enchanting from a distance than close at hand. The theaters have lost much of their former splendor. The art of music, the art of song, no longer flourish as they once did, and the future does not look promising for Italian singers. The works of the masters are utterly exhausted, and one sees no young talent emerging to replace them. Now, if we descend from the general to the particular, if we compare the fate of artists in Italy with that of our own in France, oh, my dear Euzet! It obviously takes courage and a lot of willpower to get a bit of reputation here that seems more valuable than it is, or at least fails to repay what it cost.

When you have made a successful debut here, do you know what will be asked of you? You will have to appear five or six times a week (they rehearse in the morning, and morning and evening when there is no performance). Neither a cold nor hoarseness carries any weight. Unless you are running a fever you will not be excused. So much for the throat. As for memorization, they hardly give you time to think of anything except your roles. During my eight months in Naples before my debut, I learned six roles in Donizetti operas, and I shall probably leave this country without having sung a single one. Everything is run from day to day. You never know in advance what you will be called upon to do, especially here, where the rigors of censorship may at any moment put an end to the projects of directors and composers. . . .

It is difficult to be happy away from one's own country, above all, when one has had the good fortune to be born and to live in France. But I am wrong, no doubt, to give way to such thoughts, and I fear I run a great risk of being unjust. I should not be ungrateful toward a country that has welcomed me with hospitality.

Do not think, however, that I have gone overboard in describing the fate of artists who embrace an Italian career. You have [Henri-Bernard] Dabadie[11] near you, who can tell you if I have deceived myself. Think it over before deciding to leave France for Italy.[12]

How the customs of Italian opera routine affected Nourrit immediately and intimately is further reflected in a letter to his sister, Mme Aucoc, dated 23 January 1839.

Things are not going as I should like. A singer's life in Italy is so different from a singer's life in our country. The work, the conventions, the directors, even the public, all are so little like what I knew in France for sixteen years that I have trouble adapting myself to this way of doing things. The work of memorization, above all, bothers me. Accustomed as I was to learning one or two roles a year, to taking rehearsals in my stride, to resting when I was tired, to sparing myself when I was hoarse or had a cold, I am stunned by what is required of me here (and in all Italian theaters; the San Carlo is the most accommodating in that respect): to rehearse every day, to get a new role in my head every month, never to know one day what I am to sing the next. Hardly to be certain in the morning what one will be called upon to do in the evening, and not to be excused for anything short of fever!

You see what a life that must be for one who can never make up his mind about things, who worries easily, and who cannot listen to small talk when he has to perform before the public. I may be able to adjust in time, and all this may be a good exercise to make me more philosophical, more relaxed, less intense, less thin-skinned. So let me accept all the problems as a lesson, a necessary test. Let me smother my regrets, impose silence upon my desires, and pursue courageously the route I have chosen. Since all those who love me are of the opinion that I should remain in Italy, I shall do so, and await with patience that it may please God to deliver me from exile and lead me to the promised land.

You will understand, dear sister, why I have not written more frequently. I am often short of time, and then I have to choose the right moment. I have to let pass those moments of depression that would inevitably be reflected in my letters.

I still have made no decisions for next year, and despite the monotony of the repertoire in Naples, despite the fickleness of the public, despite its coldness, I think it remains the city that will suit me best. Everywhere else they want me to commit myself to singing four times a week. As this is for seasons in which the number of performances is counted, there is no escaping the obligation. And then, I am given no assurance of new roles. To do no more than I do in Naples, to earn no more money, to expose myself to the emotional stress of a debut—it's not worth the bother. If, in Naples, I have a lot of memorizing to do, I at least have to perform less frequently, and that is so much better for the voice. I know full well that the variable climate of Naples, the sea air, the continual changing of the wind, are not favorable to the voice. But I'm beginning to get used to it, and I know not what I might find elsewhere.

I am awaiting one last reply from Milan before signing with Barbaja. Above all, I want to wait until I have sung a third opera. If *Norma*, which I am now rehearsing, is as big a success for me as *Il giuramento*, and better than *Elena*, that will make it easy for me to decide to remain here. Moreover, what do I want? I want successes that will resound in France, and I hardly think that such theaters as those of Lucca, Ancona, or Sinigaglia will bring me much glory in France.

I hear on all sides that I make new conquests of the public every day. I am always well received. Above all, I have behind me the nobility and all high society, even the king, who applauds me every time he comes to the theater. That does not prevent my half-price performances from being even more successful. So, I have nothing to complain about in that quarter. When I speak of the coldness and fickleness of the Neapolitan public, I refer simply to its reputation. If I should have to experience it myself, could I not bring myself

to accept a trial that is greater than any I have endured?
Patience![13]

Ten days later, on 5 February, Nourrit wrote to a friend,
Louis Quicherat, his future biographer, in a similar vein, but
in more explicit detail and without the fraternal restraint that
had inhibited his giving his sister a candid revelation of his
situation.

I must ask the indulgence of my friends these days. If I have
not written to them, it is because they have been too much on
my mind. Despite the glory of success at the San Carlo, I find
my decision to live thus in exile difficult. Each day I measure
the time and the distance that separate me from you. It
makes me so sad that I haven't the heart to talk of my troubles with those who love me. It is true that I am often
ashamed of my sadness, for I feel I should be thanking God
for all the good fortune he sends me. Well, despite what my
good sense tells me in that regard, I give in to the suscepti-
bilities of my troubled spirit, and cannot enjoy a ray of sunshine without thinking of the rain to come.

So, the day after my debut in *Il giuramento*, the day after
the most splendid success a French singer could hope for in
Italy, I was tormented by the fear of being unable to sustain
that success, and it must be said that the repertoire I was offered seemed to justify that fear. The role I had to accept in
Mercadante's *Elena* [*da Feltre*] suited me neither as singer
nor actor. I had, moreover, no confidence in the work itself,
which had been mounted only at the request of the prima'

donna [Giuseppina Ronzi de Begnis][14] and the baritone [Paolo Barroilhet].[15] Well, the prima donna and the baritone had a fiasco, while I alone emerged from the affair with flying colors. This success may have meant more to me than that of *Il giuramento*. In effect, I was happy to have drawn profit from that which could have done me harm. But I was no longer delighted, no longer at peace with myself. What was lacking? A good role, a good work! What was lacking above all was knowing what I had to do. But with Italian impresarios, one lives from day to day, and when an impresario meets his obligations, an artist can ask nothing more of him.

Thus, after I had devoted three or four days to *La sonnambula*, it had to be set aside to cast me in the role of Raoul in [Mercadante's] *Gabrielle di Vergy*. This role was not in my voice. I had to adapt to it, and no sooner had I begun to study it than the impresario had another change of mind. Adieu Gabrielle! It is now *Norma* that must be learned. I apply myself to *Norma*. Spech is to sing it with me. But not at all! She doesn't wish to do it any more. It is to be Ronzi. Go for Ronzi. No, Ronzi turns it down. But Spech still wants none of it. How about doing [Giuseppe Persiani's] *Inez de Castro*? Good idea. Ah, bah! No one wants it. Wait, we'll go back to *Norma*. Ronzi agrees to sing it.

You know what the tenor role is in *Norma*. Well, well, I'm reduced to relishing this role of Pollione. But as I am given only twelve days to get it in my head, I am haunted by the thought that I may not be ready. In fact, the day before the performance arrives, and I am not sure of my memory. On top of that, having learned the role more with my eyes than with the piano, I fear that it isn't in my voice. I sing Pollione, and in that role, where all the tenors have come to grief in Naples, I produce an effect surpassing all that I have achieved here. This opera, which had been howled down the last two times it was given (the public was so tired of it), has just succeeded like a new work. Is that not something to make me proud and happy? Why am I not content?

It is because art as one hears it here gives me no satisfaction. It is because I see no future for myself in an Italian career. I see no likelihood of having roles written for me. There are no composers in whom I have any confidence. To please the Italians I have to adopt a certain kind of sonority that one cannot acquire except by sacrificing the fine and delicate nuances that permit a variety of effects and give each role a distinctive character. If I persist in the system of bella voce and nothing but bella voce, I fear I may lose qualities that I prize, and that we still esteem in France, even at the Théâtre-Italien.

Another problem is that the Neapolitan climate does not suit my voice. In one day the four seasons pass in review, affecting my voice in ways that I can't account for, and that troubles me. One day it is rest that I need to be in good voice. The next day I have to work excessively hard to be well disposed. Today I have to rest at home. Tomorrow I must breathe fresh air. And so I have firmly decided not to prolong my stay here.

Unfortunately, I am having trouble coming to terms with the impresarios in other cities, who wish me to commit myself to sing at least four times a week, and who do not wish to commit themselves to giving me new roles. I have just received new proposals from Florence which appeal to me greatly, and I hope that we can reach agreement with the impresario. But what does he want me to sing? *Il giuramento* and *Robert le diable* in Italian. That will not take me one step further in my new career. But then, you are all agreed that I should remain in Italy, and I do not wish to go against the opinion of those who love me. I am profoundly convinced, however, that if I have any chance of prolonging my career for another few years, it cannot be in Italian opera. Having no possibility of returning to Paris with an entirely new repertoire, I shall not expose myself to shouldering the heritage of Rubini. I do not feel capable of struggling against the memories which that fellow will leave in the roles in which he has been heard. As far as French opera is concerned, I can think only of a new theater, there being nothing for me at the Opéra. I have no taste for taking on my old roles. If I spend much more time in Italy, moreover, my voice will have undergone such a transformation that it would be impossible for me to do so.

That's how things stand, dear friend. If I were alone, it would hardly trouble me, but I must think of the future of my family, and you will understand that it is not enough to be happy simply for today. Uncertainty as to the future prevents

my enjoying the present. . . . Ask your brother to excuse me
for not having written to him. I want two days of good spirits
in order not to risk burdening him with my jeremiads.[16]

Nourrit could spare family and friends in Paris his jeremiads, but not, inevitably, his wife, who in a letter to her
brother dated 6 February penned a jeremiad of her own.

Adolphe has felt the disadvantages of the system Donizetti
had him adopt. He has tried to return to his own, but cannot.
His head voice is gone, and his mezza voce is gone. He is
obliged to remove the few head tones he had introduced in *Il
giuramento*, and he can't sing those that are properly there in
Norma. That doesn't make much difference here. The public
doesn't ask for delicacies. The role is too low. Adolphe is
forcing his voice. He is darkening [covering] it as Donizetti
required, and he gets better results than in *Il giuramento*. I
think this is his greater success as a singer.

Does the change in voice come from the climate? Or from
the method? He will know the answer to that only after he has
left Naples. I think there is something of both, but rather
more from the method than the climate. Duprez and the Italian singers of today would suggest as much. Furthermore, it
is nothing new that the development of the chest voice ex-
tinguishes the head voice and the half-voice. Rubini almost
never uses the chest voice.

Adolphe probably knew all this. So it is not for his present
hesitation, nor for his reluctance, that I reproach him. I go

back much farther. It is rather for the illusions that he accepted and that have guided him for six months. I reproach him for the modesty that made him subject himself entirely to the judgment of Donizetti, whose artistic sensibility is far less developed than his. I reproach him for that unfortunate idea of transformation and progress that has taken hold of him, when everything around him should have told him that there is nothing but decadence in what is being done in Italy now. Yes, I believe very strongly that music is dying in Italy, just as the other arts have already died. A genius would have to come along to save it, along with several performers to herald the changes.

You will say that I believed Adolphe should come to Italy. That is true. But my first thought was that he should make no decision until he had visited Italy and seen for himself what was being done and what could be done. I would have wished him to sing only if he could have done so in his own way, and if he could have had roles other than those being performed here. But none of that was possible. He went ahead blindly. He tried to change himself at his age, when his gray hairs showed how exhausting the fifteen years of his career had been because of the nature of the roles he sang and because of the way he played them and the emotions he felt.

I know that he made up his mind only on the basis of *Polyeucte*, which Donizetti had agreed to create for him. And, indeed, his position today would have been quite different had he sung it. His success would have been such that many things would have become easy for him. And then, if the subject matter of *Polyeucte* had been accepted, the same would have been true of other roles he has in mind, and he would not have had to go through these three months of cruel anguish that impaired his resources, destroyed his calm, and undermined his confidence and the happiness he had hitherto found in the exercise of his art.

Now he is always worried, upset, and unhappy. Nothing satisfies him. The letters he receives from Paris telling of the confidence people have in him and his future do him more harm than anything else. These successes you seem to ask of him, that you seem to expect, the glory you speak of, all frighten him. The need to think constantly of the effect he must produce, and must make every effort to produce, crushes him. He sees that you are expecting a series of triumphs, and thinks that when he returns to Paris he will be unable to satisfy all that you and the public expect of him. For myself, I think that much of what you write to him is intended to combat his tendency toward discouragement. But reckonings based on normal self-satisfaction don't work with him, as he is particularly modest in his desires and in his own opinion of himself. You must, therefore, give him by way of praise and hope only what is designed to encourage him. Don't go to the point of exalting him.[17]

A day later, on 7 February, Nourrit wrote a letter to his father-in-law similar to the letter to Quicherat but with significant additional details. Having repeated what he had told his friend about *Norma*, he continued:

My God, what could I not accomplish if only I were able to have works written for me on command. But that is a hope I must abandon. There is no one in Italy but Mercadante, who writes an opera a year. Besides, the theaters in Italy are run in such a way that composers and singers don't meet or establish any contact until the moment when rehearsals begin. Then one has time only quickly to learn one's role. There can be no thought of modifying it or improving it. Ah, my poor father! Art in Italy is no longer as we think of it in France, and music in this country goes the way of painting, sculpture, and the other arts!

I await impatiently the response from Florence. Their proposal appeals to me. As to *Robert le diable*, I now accept it with pleasure. If Meyerbeer does not agree to come and stage it, I shall be sad. But we shall go ahead and make the cuts without him. . . .

I still hope to mount [Hérold's] *Zampa*, despite Barbaja's putting some obstacles in my way. He is forever at me about signing with him for a new engagement. But I do not wish to do so until I have sounded out a public other than that of Naples.[18]

In a letter of 14 February to a friend identified only as A. D., bringing him up to date with the state of his affairs in Naples, Nourrit concludes:

That, dear friend, is what concerns me, for I find it difficult to live thus from day to day. I am no longer a young man. I have to budget my time. Ah, fame is all very well, but when purchased at the price of one's peace of mind and happiness, it's too much. I often find myself longing for retirement, enjoying the fate of those who can sit in the shadows and not have to account for their activities to anyone but themselves and God. And then, one thing frightens me. I have ideas that I believe are good, but don't know, here, to whom I can impart them. Instead of growing, these ideas are wasting away, and I have reached a point where I attach less value to them every day. I feel that my spirit is losing its resilience and, also, that I am losing confidence in myself. Where will it all end?

I finish without telling you why I destroyed two letters to you that I had begun. It was because I allowed myself to go too far in speaking to you of my sadness. I shall not reread this one for fear that it may join the two others. Do I need to suggest that you not tell my mother how sad I am?[19]

Nevertheless, he covered much the same ground in a letter to his mother a week later, concluding as follows:

All goes well as far as health is concerned, but we are a long way from knowing what we are to do. The project for Florence [*Robert le diable*] having fallen through, I see four months ahead of me without an engagement. Barbaja has made his plans without me, which I should not regret, as I need to get away from Naples in order to assess the state of my voice, which here is too subject to attacks of hoarseness. . . .

Meanwhile, for the immediate future, this is the plan we have worked out—if nothing comes along to change it, since we live from day to day, and that suits me not at all. We are thinking of leaving Naples at the end of March or early April and making a short tour of northern Italy. We shall stop for a few days in Rome, Florence, Bologna, and Milan. Perhaps it may be possible to negotiate with an impresario on the spot. If that last recourse fails me, I shall take Adèle to be with Mme Ch—t at Loulans.[20] Adèle will remain there for a month while I continue on alone to Paris to look around a bit for myself and to see what I can hope for there in the near future. If I have secured an engagement with some impresario for the autumn and the carnival, I shall return with you, and either we shall take Adèle there, or she must make her own arrangements. If not, I shall return to fetch Adèle, then return with her to Paris, never again to leave, seeking to find there the best position possible.

This last decision will strike you as a desperate move, and yet we are guided by nothing but sheer necessity. The organization of the theaters in Italy is such that I can earn a little money only at the risk of losing my voice. I cannot count on making any money on the side. There being no new repertoire, I cannot think of replacing Rubini. The operas they are doing here, moreover, have hardly a chance of success in Paris. An Italian career offers me no future, and does not please me enough to justify the fatigue to which it exposes me.

In Paris lies the goal to which I aspire, but I understand that I can return only to do something new. It will take me some time to find a new position there, whatever it may be. Having no engagement for the spring or summer, how better can I occupy myself than in making a reconnaissance of the terrain? My presence may well change things, and open up possibilities of which one could have no idea from a distance, since I have already responded to all the offers made me. I want to visit Paris before committing myself to a reappearance there.

And then, I tell you again, I must leave Naples in order to recover my voice and my spirits. I have had to purchase my success with too many annoyances, and with the future promising me no better opportunities than the past, I have nothing to regret. I am busy with a bad opera [Mercadante's *Gabriella di Vergy*] and with a bad prima donna [Pixis]. I am certain that singer and opera will have a fiasco, and there is nothing to save me from the free-for-all. But, thank God, the success of *Norma* permits me to face the collapse of *Gabriella*.

That's how things stand today. We may have changed our plans in a few days, but I doubt it. God alone is Master of events, and we have good cause to resort to Him to sustain our courage. Finally, we are all well, and with health one can set things right.[21]

A week later, on 28 February, Nourrit wrote to his father-in-law:

We have been without letters for some days, and we need something to arrive from abroad to give us a bit of satisfaction. For some time, now, we have not lacked for troublesome subjects. From what I know of Barbaja, I doubt that we shall have the sadness of parting as good friends. I had, today, the proof that his tactic is always to demolish in the eyes and ears of the public those artists who have decided to leave Naples. He has flatly refused me *Zampa*, which he had promised me, and even said that he had got clearance for *William Tell*, but did not wish to give it to me as I was leaving (between ourselves, I don't believe that he got the clearance). Finally, he wants to force me to sing in Mercadante's *Gabriella*, a mediocre piece composed some twelve years ago, in the old style, an opera that the composer himself begged Barbaja not to put on. But Barbaja insists on mounting it for more than one reason. He wants first to get rid of a bad prima donna, who is to make her debut in this opera, and as it is certain that she will fail, he wants to drag me into the disaster. Since he has no more subscribers and no further commitment to the public, and since nothing is done during Lent, he has no reason to offer something good that would bring him no profit. . . .

Now that I have decided to return to France, it is important that my Neapolitan success remain intact, for my own sake as well as for the sake of others. There is no sacrifice I would not make to preserve the favor of the public and to guard against my own demoralization. Adèle has told you of the frequent recurrences of my hoarseness, and of the trouble it causes me. You know that I had to sing at court, and that the day I sang I was far from being in good voice. None of that was designed to raise my spirits. I shall, however, have to take advantage of that hoarseness to get out of *Gabriella*. Yesterday we were unable to finish the rehearsal of that opera because of the state of my voice. That state is not, I think, alarming. It's very much like what I went through in Marseilles. When I have left Naples it will be all over. But I badly need to leave Naples.[22]

The letter continues with a résumé of travel plans, and turns to the wistful thought that Nourrit's example may deter others thinking of coming to Italy.

You tell me, or others will: "You knew all that before reaching your decision." And I shall reply that I deceived myself. Perhaps my example may save other artists from the Italian sickness. I know full well that not every singer takes his calling as seriously as I do. That is, I agree, impossible in Italy. But it is also impossible for me to change myself. I would go mad if all year long I had to learn a new role every two or three weeks and be unable to do without the prompter. I have no regrets about what has been done, but I must consider the future, and not risk sacrificing it to stubborn pride. Let's hope that it doesn't merely go up in smoke.[23]

And then, for the first time, Nourrit mentions a problem with money:

It is going to break your heart that I must draw on my pension, but it has to be done to cover the cost of our return and living expenses until I have found a position.[24]

The next day he wrote to Cherubini, director of the Paris Conservatoire, requesting an extension of his leave (as professor) until May:

My primary concern, as also my first duty, will be to resume my class for the period that I shall be in the capital. But I cannot know how long that period will be, as I shall probably be returning to Italy. . . . I tell you again that the retention of my place there is so important in my eyes that I would sacrifice an engagement rather than risk losing it.[25]

Nourrit's last letter, written to his mother, is dated 4 March. After thanking her for a birthday gift (his birthdate was 3 March) and asking her to extend his thanks to others who had sent gifts, he continues:

I write above all to try to efface the bad impression that must have been made by my last letters. I gave in a bit too much to annoyance over *Gabriella*, and have now decided to sing it, for better or worse. This way I spare myself chicanery and disputation, and as I am not earning much money, I shall at least have done my duty.[26]

Nourrit's last public appearance was not in opera, but in a concert at the San Carlo on 7 March for the benefit of an indigent artist. Manuel García, Jr., who had arrived with his wife in Naples at the end of February, recorded this account of that concert and the events leading up to it in a letter dated 12 March:

On 6 March, in the morning, Adolphe came to visit my wife, who was indisposed. His state of despondency shocked me, and I detained him in a neighboring room, where also sat Maestro [Prospero] Selli.[27] There, in reply to our questions, he said, "Ah, my friend, I am very unhappy. I can no longer think! The very idea of singing tomorrow appalls me. I am tortured by fearsome thoughts. I can't get rid of them. I am tired of the struggle. I am very unhappy!"

I reminded him of the sources of domestic happiness he had in his precious family and in his friends; of the bright possibilities his position and his talents would offer him should he wish to abandon the theater, possibilities that, far from being conducive to discouragement, should arm him with strength and confidence for the future. He agreed, and finished by admitting that the distress he was suffering was only in his imagination. Having been spoiled by the good fortune of fifteen years, his spirit was not prepared for struggles. The unpleasantness he suffered went too deep not to leave scars. Finally, he said, his physical and moral strength was exhausted.

In fact, the setbacks he had suffered in being unable to practice his art in accordance with the high ideals that had made his name, the necessity of changing and diminishing his genre to the level of the routine obtaining in Italy, the incredible efforts he made to learn in a few months many roles in a foreign language, and having to appear in them for better or worse—all that had demanded so much of his mental powers that for the moment they were depleted. His body, moreover, had been weakened by an indisposition that lasted several months and considerably irritated his nervous system.

I pointed out to him that his engagement came to an end in two weeks, and that thereafter he could make a decision more to his advantage. I begged him to seek the solace of his friends, who by distractions would change the train of his thoughts and help him through this fateful time. He appeared to welcome such consolation, but when he came to his senses, the prospect of the next day's performance seemed even more terrifying, and disconcerted him all over again.

Not knowing how to draw him from his despondency, I handed him a sheet of manuscript paper, saying: "Adolphe, let's see. Put what you have just told me to work. Give free play to your ideas. Make me a poem." He promptly took the pen, and at the end of a few moments' silence, he wrote his first four verses. After he had let me read them, he added four more. As I did not appear to be satisfied with their somber tone, he said: "My friend, they express my state of mind."

Selli, who had taken little part in the conversation, said: "Monsieur, I have heard much of your literary talents, and I would like to set one of your verses to music." Adolphe responded: "Yes, I shall write a poem, and the subject will be *Le fou par excès de bonheur* [Madness through excess of good

fortune]." He left a few minutes later. Going down the stair-
case, he said to me: "Dear Manuel, it's the nights that I
dread."

The evening of 7 March Adolphe sang in the concert, and
no one imagined that it would be his last. We entered when
some feeble applause signaled the end of a number. It was
the aria from *Norma* ["Meco all'altar di Venere"]. Soon after
came the duet from the same work ["Va crudele"] with Mme
[Almeridna] Granchi[28] [as Adalgisa]. Just as his disposition
the day before had given us cause to fear, Adolphe was half
vanquished by discouragement, and this piece, although well
sung, lacked energy. Nevertheless, a feeling of respect for
the artist prompted a number of those present to express their
approval. Unfortunately, some did not share their sentiments, and there arose a violent contention between those
who wished a recall and those who didn't. The insistence of
the former persuaded the artist to return. Despite himself,
he was forced to make clear his rejection of the applause.

I think it prudent to infer here that Nourrit interpreted the
applause, probably correctly, as either derisory or compas-
sionate or, most likely, a bit of each. This seems to be supported by what follows:

I went to his dressing room and, to my great surprise,
found him attempting to do himself bodily harm. "Wasn't it
awful, the way I sang? Were they trying to mock me with
their applause? Isn't it degrading?" I tried everything possible to persuade him of the contrary.

Mme Adèle, who was disturbed by her husband's state, and who looked forward fearfully to another twelve days of the engagement, discussed with me at length the possibility of breaking with Barbaja. She begged me, above all, to see if I could not bring about the omission of the aria from *Il giuramento*, which Adolphe still had to sing, but not to do so without consulting M. [Guillaume] Cottrau.[29] I found him in the parterre, but he did not seem to agree with Mme Nourrit. I took him behind the scenes, and it was decided to leave things as they were for this evening, and to consider Adolphe's condition the next day. After singing the aria from *Il giuramento*, Adolphe said, "I am weak, but calm. It is the first time this has happened to me when performing. It's not good." And while drinking a cup of coffee to revive, he uttered these words: "This coffee makes me sick." When we tried to encourage him by reminding him that only twelve days remained until the end of his engagement, he replied, "Ah, twelve days! It's too long!"

The last aria—he sang it with supreme energy and eloquence, and the audience gave unanimous testimony to the pleasure it had experienced. But Adolphe appeared just as mortified as before, and while his friends departed satisfied, he alone saw in this concert the sentence of death.[30]

Curiously, García, who had known Nourrit well in Paris, while referring to "an indisposition that lasted several months," makes no mention of his physical appearance. Barroilhet, the excellent French baritone who was a member of the San Carlo company, in an undated letter to Nourrit's brother-in-law after the tenor's death, does:

The inconceivable melancholia that for some time undermined Adolphe Nourrit's health assumed a degree of gravity toward the end that could not but greatly trouble his family and friends. He lost a lot of weight.[31] His skin lost much of its natural color. He grew pale, and his eyes took on a haggard look. He was often witness to the torments I endured from a persistent cold, and he felt sincerely sorry for me. "You suffer greatly, my dear Barroilhet," he would say, "but nevertheless, I would gladly exchange illnesses with you. Yours is temporary, mine eternal."

"There, there," he said, smacking his forehead in a kind of rage, "is the seat of my sickness, and I feel that it is incurable."

Stunned by the way in which these words were uttered, I tried to calm him by persuading him that his sickess was all in his imagination, and that if it were not, he should consult a physician and place himself under his care, that he owed it to himself, to his family, and to his art.

One day, Dr. [Francesco] Rocca was with me when Adolphe came to call, and, alarmed by his agitation, the doctor asked him what he felt. Rocca was convinced by what Nourrit told him that he was suffering from a liver ailment that should be treated most urgently, as this type of ailment could affect the brain and have the gravest consequences.

Nourrit was impressed by what the doctor had said. The latter advised him to submit to a generous application of leeches and, if necessary, to a proper bleeding. Adolphe seemed disposed to accept this advice, but whether through negligence or distraction, he did nothing.[32]

Quicherat, in the appendices to his three-volume biography, cites a conversation between Nourrit and a friend, Guglielmi (almost certainly Guillaume [Guglielmo] Cottrau), as given in the book *Moeurs italiennes* (Italian Manners) by Paul Desmarie (1860), noting that Desmarie was drawing upon an account originally given in the journal *Omnibus pittoresco* in its issue of 28 March 1839:

On 7 March, the day before his death, one of his friends, Guglielmi, went to see him. Guglielmi found him sad and preoccupied. After some small talk, Nourrit cried out:

"Is it not true, my dear Guglielmi, that I am losing my voice? No, I cannot fulfill the task that I undertook."

"Don't you know, my dear Adolphe," Guglielmi replied, "that there's only one school in the world, the truth? It made you great in France, and it will make you great in Italy."

"No, I will never succeed in becoming an Italian singer. I am no longer what I was at the Opéra. I can no longer carry an audience with me as I could in Paris. I speak a language that is simply not my own. They hear a language that they don't understand."

"Can you complain of the Neapolitan public's welcome? Have you not been feted in the theater and in the press with unprecedented enthusiasm? Ah! if France has given us a great artist, Italy will make him still greater."

"No, the warm welcome was from pity, a matter of generosity from nation to nation. France honors all the Italian artists. Italy does not wish to do less for a poor French artist. But I cannot represent two nations. I feel there (striking his forehead) a consuming fire, and I am losing my mind— My poor children. If I go mad!— The madhouse, is it in Naples or beyond?"

"What are you saying! What an idea!"

"No, no, I want to know where the madhouse is. Out of town? Far?"

"No, not far from here."

"Very good. My wife and children will be able to visit me."

"Well then, if you truly feel sick, why not stop singing? Thank heaven, your reputation is great enough to satisfy your pride, your self-esteem, and you have twenty other ways of earning enough money to live honorably."

"Yes, that is true. But what will my enemies say? They will say that if he doesn't sing, it's because he can't. Don't you understand, my dear Guglielmi? Ah! Rather death. It's sing or die. But tonight, it's impossible—those fragments— No! I can't do it."

"But the concert is for the benefit of a poor artist."

"True, well, all right. I shall sing to their hearts' content. Am I not a poor artist? My family has no one in this world but me."

"And so, tonight?"

"Yes, tonight."

Nourrit takes his coat, passes his hand a few times across his brow as if pursuing an important thought, and says:

"I suffer much."

Then, rising suddenly, he dashes off to Barbaja and tells him: "I sing tonight— A poor artist— I must sing— I can't— But I shall."

Comes the evening. He declares himself incapable of singing. He weeps like a baby. His wife tries in vain to restore his courage. He arrives at the theater. At the sight of the audience he becomes his old self. He sings. He is sublime. Then, backstage, he is overcome by doubt. He shakes. An audience of thousands applauds in vain, recalling him to the stage. He rejects them, despite himself. Pale, haggard, wavering, he takes as derision the acclamations heaped upon him, and seems ready to fall to his knees.[33]

The following morning, five days after his thirty-seventh birthday, having slept badly or not at all, Nourrit left his bed before dawn, climbed the stairs to the top floor of the Villa Barbaja, and threw himself to his death in the courtyard below.

A funeral service was held the next day in the church of San Francesco, and Nourrit was buried in the cemetery of the Madonna del Pianto. All Naples was in shock, and because of the short notice given of the first service, a second was held on 14 March in the church of Santa Brigida.

It was, however, Mme Nourrit's wish that her husband's mortal remains accompany her back to Paris, and so it was arranged. Her brother joined her in Naples, and they journeyed to Rome, arriving there on 13 April, then embarked immediately from Civita Vecchia for Marseilles. Nourrit's body was transported separately to the French port.

There, a memorial service was held on 24 April in the church of Notre-Dame-du-Mont. As it happened, Chopin and George Sand were stopping in Marseilles at the time, on their way back from the disastrous winter in Majorca, staying out of the public eye. This was not easy, as they had been unable to find a suitable villa, and had to make do with the Hotel Darse, where as coincidence would have it, Nourrit had stayed during his fateful visit to Marseilles almost two years earlier.

For this occasion, however, Chopin made an exception, volunteering his services as organist, and playing Schubert's "Die Sterne," one of several Schubert songs that Nourrit had introduced to France. It was one of Schubert's last songs, composed in January 1828 to a poem by Karl Leitner. Curtis Cate, in his *George Sand: A Biography* (1975), gives this account, drawing on Sand's correspondence:

Their stay in Marseilles was unexpectedly saddened by the news that their old friend Adolphe Nourrit, once the star of the Paris Opéra, had committed suicide in Naples. His body reached Marseilles on 19 April, to be buried five days later.

At the request of his widow, Chopin agreed to play the organ for the funeral Elevation on exodus, but he almost lived to regret it. For the choir sang off-key, while the organ wheezed terribly. Outwitting the local gossips who flocked into the church expecting to see her "seated on the catafalque" . . . George hid away in the organ loft, where her "little one" (Chopin) valiantly strove to limit the sonic damage by avoiding the high-pitched tubes and concentrating on the deeper notes.[34]

Local dignitaries and townspeople were well aware that they were participating in the last act of a tragedy of which the first act had taken place in Marseilles.

A further memorial service was held in Lyons, and a final one in Paris at the Church of St. Roch to the music of Cherubini's Requiem, with Duprez among the soloists. Nourrit finally came to rest beside his father in the family plot in the cemetery of Montmartre.

Adèle did not long survive her beloved Adolphe. She died on 8 August 1839, five months to the day after her husband's suicide. A son, Alexis-Adolphe, was born on 6 July and died on 20 December.

Epilogue

RIDDLE ME THIS

It would seem impossible to read the foregoing without experiencing a sense of perplexity, not in one respect, but in several.

The most immediate is the matter of the tenor's health, physical as well as mental—the two quite probably related—and his apparent ignorance, in both senses of the word, of what ailed him. He had been, in fact, a very sick man for at least a year and a half before his death, probably longer. The autopsy revealed a seriously diseased liver, an enlarged heart, and diseased intestines, with evidence of chronic dysentery accompanied by discharge of mucous and blood.

In his letter to Féréol of 22 November 1837, he tells how his physican "dosed me up solidly in order to get rid of both the cold and *the colic* [italics added]." He continued: "Thus, I have spent the last two weeks by the fireside, taking barley water, sulphur water, pills, potions, and enemas. I have even treated myself to some fifteen leech applications and one vesication. But my condition remains about the same."[1]

And so, with his physician's approval, he set off in the dead of winter for northern Italy for rest, recuperation, and reconnaissance! Anyone who has spent winters in Italy—

and I spent two with the American Fifth Army during World War II, one in the south near Naples and Cassino, the other in the mountains between Florence and Bologna—will agree that a less judicious decision could hardly have been made, especially since, by purpose and design, it involved constant travel by coach, including the hazardous traversal of the Maritime Alps between Turin and Genoa (twice) and the Appenines between Bologna and Florence, not to mention the initial journey to Turin.

It should be noted in the physician's defense that he may have been influenced by the conventional image of "sunny Italy" and unaware of a wintertime Italy that can be anything but sunny. In all other respects the approval was wise. It got Nourrit out of Paris, where, unable to perform, he would have been miserable, and gave him not only a beneficial change of scene, but also a new goal and, for about a year, a new lease on life. It remains odd, however, that his physician seems not to have advised him to seek at least periodic medical consultation.

And yet, from the time of his arrival in Turin on 16 December 1837, to his death fifteen months later, the correspondence contains no reference to problems of health beyond those of colds and hoarseness. Even his wife's letters to the family in Paris after she had joined him in Naples in June, though they speak, toward the end, of his depressed mental state, mention no physical symptoms beyond colds and hoarseness and being in bad voice.

Then, two days before his death, Nourrit visited his old friend Manuel García, Jr., recently arrived with his wife in

Naples, and García was shocked by his state of despondency. In his letter of 12 March 1839, following the tenor's suicide, García wrote: "His body, moreover, had been weakened by *an indisposition that lasted several months and considerably irritated his nervous system* [italics added]."[2]

Even García passed over what must surely have been the most obvious evidence of something gravely amiss: Nourrit's physical appearance. This is noted only in the letter written by Nourrit's colleague, the baritone Barroilhet, to the tenor's brother-in-law after his death:

> The inconceivable melancholia that for some time undermined Adolphe Nourrit's health assumed a degree of gravity toward the end that could not but greatly trouble his family and friends. He lost a lot of weight. His skin lost much of its natural color. He grew pale, and his eyes took on a haggard look.[3]

This reads much like the description given of his appearance after the abortive provincial tour eighteen months earlier. Barroilhet's physician, Dr. Rocca, immediately noted that there was more at the root of Nourrit's condition than melancholia and, indeed, that melancholia could well be a symptom rather than a cause. He diagnosed the problem as a liver ailment, and prescribed a course of treatment similar, in fact, to what Nourrit had undergone in Paris.

The mystery remains. Nourrit must have known, if only from the treatment in Paris, not to speak of something as obvious as chronic dysentery, that something was seriously wrong. His wife must have known. But there is no record, no suggestion, of his ever having sought medical advice or treatment, or of his wife's having urged him to do so.

Matters of health aside, Nourrit's going to Italy to master the new Italian style was, as his wife subsequently observed, a rash decision for one who was not only at the height of a glorious career, but who was also thirty-five years old, with a voice already exposed to sixteen years of singing some of the most exacting and exhausting roles in the tenor repertoire, many of them roles he created.

In terms of the new direction that the opera genre could be seen to be taking, the decision made sense. What is more difficult to fathom is Nourrit's determination to think in terms of a future in Italy rather than France, especially since he reached that decision when extensive travel in Italy had left him with a more than adequate insight into the slovenly management and routine and the meager repertoire of even the better houses.

Italian colleagues in Paris could have enlightened him without his ever leaving town, but obviously he did not see fit to solicit their advice. He probably feared that a display of curiosity would arouse their suspicions about what had prompted it and excite curiosity on their part as to what he had in mind.

The prospect of making a debut in Naples in a new opera written especially for him by Donizetti was understandably irresistible. But it need not have persuaded him to accept an engagement by Barbaja as a member of the Neapolitan company. The success and prominence denied him by the censors' rejection of *Poliuto* were partially compensated for by his subsequent success in *Il giuramento*. But that success left him, in a sense, high and dry.

With Donizetti now committed to Paris, neither Mercadante nor any other composer had anything similarly congenial to offer. Nourrit should have been able to see that, while his success in *Il giuramento*, and subsequently as Pollione in *Norma*, made him a desirable acquisition for other Italian houses, none of them would or could offer him a congenial repertoire in a congenial working environment.

One of his reasons for deciding as he did is the most baffling element of all, namely, his appallingly naive conviction that, by his example, he could single-handedly elevate Italian taste and introduce Italy to a new and better operatic era and climate. In this he was led astray by his own idealism, enthusiasm—and vanity. He had been in the theater long enough, even in Italy, to know better.

Nourrit, as singing actor, was one of the greatest tragedians of his time, possibly of any time. But the greatest tragedy he played was the one for which he could take no curtain calls.

Postscripts

DIAGNOSIS IN RETROSPECT

I am indebted to my late friend William B. Ober, the eminent American pathologist and essayist, for the following retrospective diagnosis of Nourrit's ailments as suggested by the disclosures of the autopsy. For the subsequent evaluation of Nourrit's psychiatric condition, thanks are due to the esteemed Joseph H. Stephens, associate professor of psychiatry at The Johns Hopkins University School of Medicine in Baltimore, Maryland.

Nourrit's Physical Condition
by William B. Ober, M.D.

The chronic dysentery was probably what we now call chronic idiopathic ulcerative colitis. It is a profoundly debilitating disease. On symptomatic grounds one cannot distinguish between it and granulomatous enterocolitis (either idiopathic or tubercular), but ulcerative colitis is often accompanied by fatty degeneration of the liver, whereas the granulomatous forms are not. A year and a half of frequent bloody stools, plus advancing liver disease, are sufficient to serve as an organic basis for mental depression and suicide.

Today we treat ulcerative colitis with steroids with some success. Before that it was not uncommon to treat it by surgical resection of the colon and a permanent ileostomy. But neither surgery nor steroids were available in the 1830s.

It is a disease that can occur at any age, but the peak incidence is between twenty and forty-five. I have seen it occur as early as fourteen and as late as ninety, but it is predominantly a disease of young adults. The autopsy also showed an enlarged heart, but I do not know what caused this, and I do not think that it was related to the colitis and the fatty liver. Nourrit was obese and may have had hypertension, but that was in the days before we could measure blood pressure by the sphygmomanometer.

Like all retrospective diagnoses, the foregoing is what I would call an educated guess. The retrospectoscope is the perfect medical instrument. One can never prove it wrong— or right.

Nourrit's Psychiatric Condition
by Joseph H. Stephens, M.D.

All retrospective psychiatric diagnoses made only on the basis of surviving letters and other documents are of course suspect. In 1984 the American Psychiatric Association published the third revision of its *Diagnostic and Statistical Manual of Mental Disorders* (*DSM III*) in an effort to bring order to the lack of standardization in diagnostic usage. In 1994 *DSM IV* was published, and there are still skeptics who have suggested it would be more useful to classify the clas-

sifiers than to classify the classifier's diagnoses. Nevertheless *DSM IV* is currently the bible of diagnosis.

Dr. Ober's suggestion that Nourrit's one and a half years
of bloody stools and advanced liver disease are sufficient to
justify the diagnosis "organic basis for mental depression
and suicide due to gastrointestinal and liver disease" (*DSM
IV* 293.83) seems a less persuasive diagnosis than "major
depressive disorder recurrent with melancholic features"
(*DSM IV* 296.33).

In order to qualify for the second of these two *DSM IV* diagnoses, at least five of the following symptoms must have
been present for at least two weeks most of the day or nearly
every day.

1. Depressive mood most of the day nearly every day by
subjective report or observation of others.

2. Markedly diminished interest or pleasure in all or
almost all activities most of the day nearly every day.

3. Significant weight loss or gain.

4. Insomnia or hypersomnia nearly every day.

5. Psychomotor agitation or retardation nearly every day.

6. Fatigue or loss of energy nearly every day.

7. Feelings of worthlessness or excessive or inappropri-
ate guilt nearly every day.

8. Diminished ability to think or concentrate, or indecisiveness nearly every day.

9. Recurrent thoughts of death, recurrent suicidal ideation, or a suicide attempt or plan.

Clearly Nourrit exhibited all nine of these symptoms on more than one occasion and thus must be diagnosed by *DSM IV* criteria as suffering from a major depression. It is individuals with this diagnosis who are most likely to kill themselves. Suicide is most common when a person perceives his predicament as hopeless. Nourrit was surely convinced that his potential for being someone who mattered was exhausted, and his suicide seems almost inevitable in the absence of the treatment available today but not one hundred and fifty years ago.

NOURRIT AS OTHERS SAW AND HEARD HIM

England

Henry Fothergill Chorley discusses Nourrit's Robert in *Robert le diable* in volume one of his three-volume *Music and Manners in France and Germany (1841–44):*

The full brilliancy of this character has never been thoroughly brought out save by him who created it (to use the French phrase)—I do not say in full manliness—for the very elegance, so highly prized and loudly regretted by a portion of the Parisian *cognoscenti*, bordered so closely upon a mannered over-grace and over-sweetness that I never heard that fine singer, and never saw that elegant actor, without feeling that neither his clear and metallic voice—nasal in its falsetto—nor his graceful gestures belonged to the greatest school of art.

There was a smile when he threw his head back to sing, or to launch a *mot* at someone behind him, a mincing elongation of his *oui*'s and *patrie*'s and the other sounds which, sung in French, are intrinsically offensive, that annoyed my insular eyes and ears, as imparting to grace and sentiment and emphasis a touch of make-believe destructive of their effect.

He appears on recollection to have been more conscious of his handsome person and high voice and artistic accomplishments than anyone I have ever seen on the French stage, to have attitudinized more premeditatedly, to have declaimed with more of that conventional exactness which, as English ears unhappily know, can become so utterly intolerable, than the generality of his brethren, the old Roman gentlemen with their lean throats and their nonpareil toupets at the Théâtre-Français always excepted.

And yet when I think of the joyous and sparkling vivacity with which he threw off the song, "L'or est une chimère," of the enthusiasm he put forth in the chivalresque duet with Bertram, I am half tempted to draw my pen through any qualification of merits so honorable as his, because they were so largely owing to pride in his art and research into its legitimate effects. When I heard Nourrit, too, his best days had long passed. The fame of his rival [Duprez] cast its shadow before. He looked feverish and anxious, and as if he devoured the plaudits with a jealous ear, which could detect whether one hand less was raised than had acknowledged his triumphs the night before. But while the public was listening to him, it was already busily talking of Duprez. . . .

His glory had been won in stirring times. To quote an eloquent writer in *La Revue des Deux Mondes*, "he marked the transition from the old recitative of the French to the cavatina of the Italians. And yet he was so far national that, whereas the singers of the south are far too apt to sacrifice unity of character to one particular moment or favorite note, he carried his activity and care into the minutest details of his part, and from his first entrance to his final exit never ceased to *be* the person he represented."

Costume, attitude, by-play, nothing was neglected by Nourrit. Hence he might be the darling of people to whom mere musical emotions will not compensate for want of interest in the drama, want of tact in the actors, want of taste in the *mise en scène*; hence he might well be endowed with an importance and authority which his performances so eminently sustained.

Nor were his interests confined to music. M. Berlioz tells us that his strong and visionary enthusiasm led him to project schemes of a religious theatrical reform, for the purification and elevation of the stage. He had visions of human perfectibility. He was sincerely ambitious to bear his part in advancing human progress.

To such a man so placed, organized, moreover, by nature with the acutest possible sensibilities, the idea of rivalry must have been intolerable torment. He could not be expected to admit that the very revolution in which he had been bearing a part must lead to developments in art at which he must stop short, to requisitions from the public which there was no chance of his satisfying. Nor could he be expected to admit that a more graceful and rhythmical and melodious school of music must superinduce the necessity of artists who should be more largely and richly singers than he, with all his dramatic care and vocal agility, had been. [Nourrit's letters tell us otherwise. H. P.]

For Nourrit to enter into competition with a younger man, and thus own that his supremacy was no longer unquestioned, was impossible. Perhaps, too, he felt instinctively that the wear and tear of an immense stage and a powerful orchestra for fourteen successive years had told their tale upon him. The anecdotes of the conflict and distress of mind he endured, now religiously treasured by the Parisians as the relics of a martyr, are very painful and, to our eyes, strange.

His melancholy fate has led his countrymen into the lengths of a fond injustice. I have heard not a few Parisians speak of Duprez in a resentful and disparaging tone, as though *he* had been the cause of the tragical catastrophe.

We order matters differently in England. No changes of Time or Fashion are allowed to push our old favorites from their stools. We will not admit that powers are impaired, or that anyone belonging to a newer dynasty of art can possess greater refinements of intelligence than those that charmed us twenty years hence!

But of our amount of regret for dead or utterly vanished greatness, it may be feared that we cannot so justly boast.[1]

Italy

Leopoldo Tarantini discusses Nourrit's Neapolitan debut in *Il giuramento* in *Salvator Rosa: Album artistico, scientifico e litterario*, 18 November 1838, here freely translated from the French translation given in Quicherat.

Il giuramento, long awaited, so often promised, has finally been given.

Simultaneously we have experienced the debut of Adolphe Nourrit, reigning tenor of the French opera scene, creator of the leading roles of *Robert le diable* and *La Juive*, and the one for whom Rossini composed *William Tell*. This young man, eager for glory, passionately devoted to his art, feted and adored in Paris, at home on the pinnacle of fame, has renounced that enviable position to pursue a glorious but very difficult future.

He wished to become a tenor in Italy, to challenge Rubini and surpass Duprez. Nourrit comes to Naples already a master. He submits to all the difficulties of apprenticeship, and the evening of the 14th [of November] was to decide whether his undertaking was noble, courageous, or rash, whether a double palm would render him an even more exalted object of envy, or whether he would collapse under the weight of his presumption. The artist was atremble, and not without reason, for at this moment two nations had their eyes fixed upon him.

Thus all were in a state of suspense when the curtain rose on this memorable evening in the history of our theater, and a magical metamorphosis was exposed to our eyes. We find ourselves confronted with a new taste, a new system. *Il giuramento* bears no resemblance to that to which we have hitherto been accustomed.

Nourrit triumphed over every difficulty and every hazard, and may now enter proudly upon the Italian scene. His voice, clear and melodious, is equally effective in forceful and tender passages. He sings his two principal arias with a suavity that suggests the divine. His high notes are very beautiful, and if, from time to time, we detect a suggestion of nasality, we note that this fault, inherent in the French voice, is conspicuous only in recitative and on certain notes in an aria. But in the grand passages, where Nourrit is able to display all his voice, he shows how well study has triumphed over habit, and how soon he will possess a perfect Italian pronunciation.

But what to say of his singing, his declamation, his acting? Truth and nature are fully reflected in his gestures. And still, the most profound art, with all its precepts, cannot suggest anything more perfect, more appropriate to the scene. When passion overtakes him, he is transported, and abandons himself to the dictates of his heart. And yet, in these transports there is nothing with which critics can find fault. The style of his declamation may be a bit too fervid, but this fervor derives from feeling, profound and true, and owes nothing to artifice. If, occasionally, Nourrit appears exalted, it is the exaltation of the man, not the actor, an exaggeration of sensibility, not of method. He never forgets himself. He always reflects the situation, and one sees the drama unfold and move toward the catastrophe without any sense of the artist's ever drawing attention to himself as a personage.

His voice and his singing always conserve that truthfulness of expression that makes us understand how generations have so venerated the names of [David] Garrick and [François-Joseph] Talma. Nourrit is an actor who sings, not a singer who acts. *Il giuramento* has been given in Milan, Turin, and Venice. The tenor role has made no impression. Here, in Naples, it has become the most important and the most prominent. Therein lies the true homage to Nourrit.

Nourrit has surpassed the expectations of the public, but the public, too, in its applause, surpassed the expectations of Nourrit, who shed tears of gratitude. On this occasion, hospitality and national glory triumphed.[2]

THE THREE TENORS OF THE 1830S

Giovanni-Battista Rubini

Half of the four-century span of opera history passed before the tenor, as a vocal category, achieved stellar status—an observation that may strike a strange note at this time in the twilight of the era dazzled by "the three tenors." The first tenor to achieve stellification was Giovanni-Battista Rubini, the bicentenary of whose birth fell in 1994 (or perhaps 1995, depending upon which reference book you consult). He was born on 7 April in the village of Romano di Lombardia, on the southern edge of the province of Bergamo.

Rubini was not the first tenor to achieve prominence performing leading roles in serious operas as opposed to comic ones, but of a group of his elder contemporaries, among whom were Giacomo David (1750–1831), his son Giovanni (1790–1864), Andrea Nozzari (1775–1832), and Manuel García (1775–1832), Rubini was the most outstanding, the most famous, the most prosperous, and the most international. He outshone them in much the same way Mario, Jean de Reszke, and Caruso would, at the height of their powers, eclipse their contemporaries—just as today Carreras, Domingo, and Pavarotti have dominated their era.

146

Although tenors were a common fixture in eighteenth-century *opera buffa,* it was Rossini who was the first to capitalize on this vocal range for *opera seria.* It can fairly be said that he was the one who released the tenor, and the bass, too, from the shadow of the male and female sopranos and male contraltos. In his first opera for Naples, *Elisabetta, regina d'Inghilterra,* he used two tenors: Nozzari as Leicester and the elder García as Norfolk. The following year, in *Otello,* he employed three: Nozzari (Otello), Giovanni David (Rodrigo), and García (Iago). When he moved to Paris, he converted the *travesti* contralto role of General Calbo into a tenor part (Néoclès) as part of his revision of *Maometto II* as *Le siège de Corinthe.*

The affinity that Bellini felt toward the tenor voice sprang from an association with Rubini's art that began in 1826 with the young composer's first publicly staged opera, *Bianca e Gernando.*[3] Rubini was in the first casts of three of Bellini's subsequent operas: *Il pirata* (Milan, 1827), *La sonnambula* (Milan, 1831), and *I Puritani* (Paris, 1835). It was Bellini who launched Rubini to unprecedented stardom, not only with his music but also, it would seem, with his tutoring or coaching. It must be acknowledged, too, that no small part of Rubini's celebrity derived from his performing music by other composers written for other tenors.

In his biography of Bellini, Herbert Weinstock quotes this account by Bellini's friend Giacomo Barbò di Castelmorano of what took place in his presence during the rehearsals of *Il pirata.* Bellini is reported to have said:

Dear Rubini, are you thinking about being Rubini or being Gualtiero? Don't you know that your voice is a gold mine that has yet to be discovered? Listen to me, and someday you will be grateful to me. You are one of the best singers. No one equals you in bravura. But that isn't enough. . . . Admit it. My music doesn't please you because it doesn't provide you with the usual opportunities. But if it has entered my head to produce a new sort of music which expresses the words very closely, and to make a unit of the words and the singing, tell me, must you be the one from whom I receive no help? You can do it. Forget yourself, and throw yourself with all your soul into the character you are representing.[4]

How profitably Rubini took this advice to heart is reflected in the critical reaction to his performance of the Tomb Scene in the first Paris production of Donizetti's *Lucia* in 1837. Of that performance Pierre Scudo wrote that "no other singer has been able to reproduce the sob of fury which Rubini emitted from his trembling mouth." Another critic, Ernest Legouvé, observed that Rubini "was suddenly transformed into a tragedian by dint of being a sublime singer."[5]

Neither critic mentions his acting, probably because there was nothing to say. Henry Chorley, writing some years after Rubini's death, sums him up in these terms:

He rarely tried to act, the moment of the curse in the contract scene of *Lucia* being the only attempt of the kind that I can call to mind. The voice and the expression were, with him, to "do it all." . . . As a singer, and nothing beyond a singer, he is the only man of his class who deserves to be mentioned in these pages as an artist of genius.[6]

One would deduce that Rubini was more singer than actor, and Adolphe Nourrit, his most significant contemporary among French tenors, was more actor than singer because the commentators mentioned Nourrit's singing as infrequently as they referred to Rubini's acting. I find myself reminded here, again and again, of Domingo and Pavarotti—the former playing Nourrit to the latter's Rubini. Domingo has been the greater artist of the two—as Nourrit was—a better actor with a far wider ranging repertoire, as might be said of Nourrit vis-à-vis Rubini. In terms simply of singing, however, in terms of the enjoyment of singing and sharing that joy with his listeners, Rubini, a century and a half ago, and Pavarotti today, have proven themselves stars.

As with Pavarotti and Domingo, so, too, Rubini and Nourrit knew and respected one another. In Paris during the 1830s Rubini belonged to the company appearing at the Théâtre-Italien, while Nourrit sang at the Opéra between 1821 and 1837. In his three-volume biography of Nourrit, Louis Quicherat gives this account of a chance meeting on a Paris street:

One day Nourrit, strolling with one of his friends, met Rubini. They exchanged a few words. Afterwards, Nourrit said to his companion: "Do you know to whom I was speaking? Ah, what an admirable talent!" "Yes," his friend replied, "he's a great singer, but as an actor he leaves much to be desired. He is often awkward on the stage." Nourrit received this criticism with a vivacity bordering on displeasure. "But," he replied, "what is missing when he sings? Is there not inspiration in his voice, pathos in his accents?"[7]

Not that Domingo and Pavarotti have ever sounded as Nourrit and Rubini did. Both the latter were, at the height of their careers, thought to be old-fashioned in style and vocalism. Rubini's singing harked back to the art of the castrati, with much use of head voice, mixed voice, and falsetto. He was a bravura singer able to negotiate formidable passages of fioritura. Nourrit, on the other hand, although he had been schooled by the elder Manuel García, sang in a way that made clear his devotion to classical French theatrical and poetic declamation that he had learned from his youthful idol, the tragedian Talma. And he, too, resorted to head voice, rather than chest resonance, above the tenor high G and A.

Both Rubini and Nourrit were to be supplanted by tenors who employed the heavier, darker, more viscerally exciting, more masculine *voix sombrée.* The elder of these new-style tenors was Domenico Donzelli (1790–1873), who sang Pollione in the premiere of *Norma;* the other was Gilbert-Louis Duprez (1806–1896), the first Edgardo in *Lucia.* When Nourrit heard Duprez sing at the Opéra he decided to go to Italy and acquire the new Italian style. He foresaw, correctly, that it would prove to be the vocal fashion of the future.

Nourrit continued with his Italian project and died in Italy in 1839, a melancholy suicide. Rubini survived, dividing his time between Paris and London, but in late 1843 he went to St. Petersburg, probably aware that, in terms of the shift in

European taste in singing, the Russians were behind the times. He was received with high honors there, named director of singing in the realm of Czar Nicholas I and designated a colonel of the Imperial Music.

He returned to Italy about 1845, retired to his birthplace, and built a handsome villa for himself and his wife, the singer Adelaide Comelli-Rubini (1796–1874). There, on 2 March 1854, he died. The villa still stands today as a Rubini museum, housing precious relics of his career, including his Russian colonel's uniform, and is well worth a visit by opera historians and aficionados of the tenor voice.

A fitting summary of the impression Rubini could produce is supplied by Henry Chorley, who had heard the tenor in each of his thirteen consecutive London seasons (1831–1843). Nineteen years after his last exposure to Rubini's vocalism, he wrote:

> [Rubini] ruled the stage by the mere art of singing more completely than anyone, woman or man, has been able to do in my time. . . . He may be said to be the last of the remarkable company of Italian tenors for whom Signor Rossini wrote. . . . The traditions of his method died with him.[8]

Adolphe Nourrit

When we use the term "dramatic tenor," it is usually to characterize a type of voice, heavier, more robust, more forceful, and more resonant than a lyric tenor. But there is an implication that the dramatic tenor should also be an actor, indeed, a tragedian, since this type of voice lends itself to the big tragic or heroic roles; and the greatest dramatic tenors have all been great actors, or have become good ones—Nourrit, Duprez, Tamberlik, Tichatschek, de Reszke, Tamagno, Campanini, Slezak, Caruso, and Martinelli. Most of them have been singers first, actors later—acting singers rather than singing actors. And since opera is primarily a singer's arena, a confrontation of the two types, assuming that the acting singer is a tolerably good actor, will usually be resolved in his favor. This was the personal tragedy of Adolphe Nourrit (1802–1839), who may well have been the greatest singing actor among all the dramatic tenors of opera history.

He was certainly the most creative. Among the roles written for him were Néoclès in *Le siège de Corinthe*, Aménophis in *Moïse*, Arnold in *William Tell*, and the Count in *Le Comte Ory*, all by Rossini; Masaniello in *La muette de Portici* and Gustave in *Gustave III*, by Auber; Éléazar in *La Juive*, by Halévy; and Robert in *Robert le diable*, and Raoul in *Les Huguenots*, by Meyerbeer. Other tenors may have created more roles, although it is doubtful. No other has created a comparable number of roles so substantial and enduring. Indeed, until Verdi and Wagner came along, it could be said that Nourrit, virtually single-handed, had made a repertoire for the dramatic tenor. And singers of so recent memory as Caruso and Martinelli could thank Nourrit for Éléazar, in which each of them found one of his most congenial roles.

Certainly, and to his sorrow, Nourrit created a repertoire for Duprez. Nourrit's reign at the Opéra lasted from 1824 to 1837, when Duprez, who had hitherto made his career in

Italy, was engaged for the Opéra and allowed to make his debut in Nourrit's role of Arnold in *William Tell*. This was too much for Nourrit. He withdrew from the Opéra and spent the remaining two years of his life touring the French provinces and Italy, while the public and the critics argued the merits of the situation and of the two tenors. Nourrit was disconsolate, feeling that the less sophisticated art of the acting singer had triumphed over his own more refined accomplishments as a singing actor. He never felt quite at home away from Paris, although he was successful enough, even in Italy. He developed symptoms of mental illness, and early in the morning of 8 March 1839, he jumped to his death from the window of his third-floor apartment in Naples.

In many respects his career had paralleled that of Wilhelmine Schröder-Devrient, who was also his contemporary. Both were born into the theater. Schröder-Devrient's mother, it will be remembered, had been known as "the German Mrs. Siddons." Nourrit's father, Louis Nourrit (1780–1831), was the leading tenor at the Opéra until succeeded by Adolphe after the latter's triumph in *Le siège de Corinthe* in 1826. While Schröder-Devrient's model had been her mother, Nourrit's was Talma, the great French tragedian. Although Nourrit studied singing with García, it used to be said of him that he "had been instructed by García, but inspired by Talma."

Talma's example led Nourrit far beyond the average actor's—or average singer's—range of intellectual curiosity and interest. He read widely, visited museums, studied the history of the theater, and became an excellent musician. He also became a good poet. The words to "Rachel, quand du Seigneur" from *La Juive*—which Jan Peerce and Richard Tucker have sung so well in our own time—were written by Nourrit, as were translations of some Schubert songs which he was the first to introduce to the public in France. Here, too, were an enthusiasm and an accomplishment that he shared with Schröder-Devrient, who might have had some reservations about hearing *Die junge Nonne* as *La jeune religieuse*. He was an imaginative, all-around man of the theater, and his advice was sought and often accepted by both Halévy and Meyerbeer.

The elder Nourrit, in addition to being the leading tenor at the Opéra, was also a diamond merchant, and it was the latter trade that he proposed for Adolphe. The result, for his son, was a late start as a singer, a handicap he never entirely overcame. Thanks to his Italian schooling under García, he was able to cope with Rossini, but aside from *Otello*, he sang only in Rossini's later French operas, all written specifically for him. Rossini, with his extraordinary gift and predilection for tailoring his music to fit an extraordinary voice, never burdened him with the virtuoso requirements he had imposed upon David, Nozzari, Rubini, and Donzelli.

Nourrit's was an agreeable, strong, and expressive voice, capable of a brilliant, though not full-voiced, high C and resourcefully employed in diminuendo, *voix-mixte, voix de tête*, and falsetto. Had he been an Italian, or had he been less concerned with the art of the actor, poet, and pantomimist, he might have been a great singer in the older Italian style. But his preoccupation with every linguistic and dramatic nuance, his excellence in declamation and recitative, his determination that every syllable and every movement should contribute to his projection of the character he was portraying, were incompatible with the Italian concentration upon an uninterrupted melodic flow. He admired the great Italian singers, even the Italian-oriented Duprez, but he found their art one-sided and lacking in those refinements of vocal shading and poetic or dramatic utterance that so distinguished his own accomplishments as singer and actor.

When he went to Italy after withdrawing from the Opéra, he tried to adapt his singing to the Italian taste and to eliminate the nasality that marred certain of his tones. Donzelli's dark quality, or *voix sombrée*, which Duprez had adopted in Italy and which had contributed to his success in Paris, was Nourrit's goal. He even achieved it. But he was disturbed by his own success. "I hoped always," he wrote to a friend from Naples, "that with time I could recover those fine nuances that were the essence of my talent, and the variety of inflection I had had to abandon in order to conform to the exigencies of Italian singing." After his debut there he wrote again: "To tell the truth, with the Italian inflection that I have cultivated, I have only one color at my disposal, and I find myself falling into precisely those errors for which we reproach the Italians."

Nourrit was a handsome man, with black curly hair, lively eyes, and an intelligent and sympathetic countenance. He was burdened with obesity, but made up for it by the lightness and propriety of his movements and by great care in the choice and cut of his clothes and costumes. His circle of acquaintances, as might have been expected in a man of such diverse interests and accomplishments, extended well beyond the confines of the theater, and included both Chopin and Liszt, who introduced him to the music of Schubert.

Chopin was staying in Marseilles when Nourrit's body was brought through on the way to Paris. There was a funeral service at the church of Notre-Dame-du-Mont on 24 April 1839, and the organist was Chopin. During the Elevation he played Schubert's "Die Sterne": "not," as George Sand wrote, "with the passionate and glowing tone that Nourrit used, but with a plaintive sound, as soft as an echo from another world."

Gilbert-Louis Duprez

One of the most engaging of Berlioz's *Evenings in the Orchestra* is a piece called "The Tenor's Revolution Around the Public, an Astronomical Study." Its hero, after initial good schooling, makes a premature Paris debut, then hies himself off to Italy. There his voice and his art develop; he does well, is exploited by all and sundry, and returns to France, where he is re-engaged. On the night of his debut:

A number comes during which the daring artist, *accenting each syllable*, gives out some high chest notes with a resonance, an expression of heart-rending grief, and a beauty of tone that so far no one had been led to expect. Silence reigns in the stupefied house, people hold their breath, amazement and admiration are blended in an almost similar sentiment, fear; in fact, there is some reason for fear until that extraordinary phrase comes to its end; but when it has done so, triumphantly, the wild enthusiasm may be guessed. . . . Then from two thousand panting chests break forth cheers such as an artist hears only twice or thrice in his lifetime, cheers that repay him sufficiently for his long and arduous labors.

All this is a reasonably accurate account of the early life and eventual Paris triumph of Gilbert-Louis Duprez (1806–1896). Berlioz goes on to give a far from flattering account of our tenor hero's ascendancy and decline. While riding high he is patronizing toward composers and jeopardizes the stability of the opera by exacting exorbitant fees. In decline he "has to decapitate every phrase and can sing only in his middle register. He plays fearful havoc with the old scores and imposes an insupportable monotony on the new ones as a condition of their existence." Finally comes a farewell appearance in *William Tell*, rather sympathetically told, and the crown passes to a new hero. . . .

Duprez had sung the title role in Berlioz's *Benvenuto Cellini* in 1838, and Berlioz, in his *Memoirs*, remembered:

Duprez was very good in any violent scene, but his voice had already ceased to lend itself to soft airs, long-drawn notes, a calm, dreamy music. For instance, in the air "Sur les monts les plus sauvages," he could not sustain the high G at the end of the phrase "Je chanterais gaiment"; and instead of holding the note for three bars as he should have done, held it for only a moment, and thus destroyed the effect.

Berlioz also remembered Duprez's habit, in the air "Asile héréditaire" in *William Tell*, of always singing an F instead of a G-flat (enharmonic F-sharp). He once asked him why. "I don't know," said Duprez, "that note puts me out. It bothers me." Duprez promised to try singing it correctly once, just to please Berlioz, but he never did. "Neither for me, nor for himself, nor for Rossini, nor for common sense," wrote Berlioz, "did Duprez ever do the G-flat in any performance of *William Tell*. Neither saints nor devils could make him give up his abominable F. He will die impenitent."

It is unlikely that Berlioz had often heard Duprez at his best. The tenor was only thirty at the time of his sensational debut at the Opéra as Arnold in *William Tell* on 17 April 1837, but he had already been singing in Italy for nearly a decade. He had created the role of Edgardo in *Lucia* in Naples in 1835—the last scene of *Lucia* gives us some idea of what kind of singer he must have been at that time—and he had sung Arnold in the Italian premiere of *William Tell* at Lucca in 1831.

It was on this latter occasion that he discovered his potential as a dramatic tenor. Until then he had been just another lyric tenor, and small-voiced at that. When he first sang at the Odéon in Paris in 1825 it was said that one had to be seated in the prompter's box to hear him. He was selected for the role of Arnold only as an emergency replacement for Benedetta Pisaroni. He knew that the kind of voice he had employed heretofore would be inadequate for the big scenes of *William Tell*, and in his own words, as recorded in his *Souvenirs d'un chanteur*, "It required the concentration of every resource of will power and physical strength. 'So be it,' I said to myself, 'it may be the end of me, but somehow I'll do it.' And so I found even the high C which was later to bring me so much success in Paris."

Duprez is referring here to the extraordinary passage in the stretta of the fourth act, following the "Asile héréditaire," in which the voice must twice ascend from G by way of A, B-flat, and B-natural to a sustained high C. It was Duprez's stentorian and electrifying delivery of this passage that secured his success and supremacy in Paris and established his place in tenor history as the first to sing the high C from the chest.

Rossini did not like it. "That tone," he used to say, "rarely falls agreeably upon the ear. Nourrit sang it in head voice, and that's how it should be sung." Rossini had first heard Duprez's high C in his (Rossini's) own home, and had expressed his opinion by looking to see if any of his precious Venetian glass had been shattered. It struck his Italian ear, he observed, "like the squawk of a capon whose throat is being cut."

Duprez must have been, as compared with Nourrit, a conspicuously limited singer. His reliance upon the *voix sombrée* inhibited his mobility in rapid passages, and he was taken to task frequently for his habit of retardation. One caustic Paris critic observed of the passage "Suivez-moi!" in this same fourth-act stretta that Duprez would not have been difficult to follow at the pace he was taking. And the high C would appear to have been his absolute top. He simply omitted the C-sharp in the second-act duet, which Nourrit had taken easily in head voice.

Duprez assessed the comparison differently, of course. Nourrit, he conceded,

> declaimed well; but his singing always impressed me as communicating less of compassion than of impetuosity and ardor. His voice had the quality of what used to be called a counter-tenor (*haute-contre*), and he could sing very high in a mixed register. When fate ruled that I should become his rival I knew perfectly well that the production of that voice, white and slightly gutteral, was totally incompatible with the method I had developed for my own. I also knew that my approach to recitative was entirely different from his and from other singers who had preceded me; for it had been their custom to *recite* rather than *sing*. They had looked upon recitative as a bridge from one vocal number to another. I, on the other hand, saw in recitative an essential element of composition, indispensable to the action and the expression, serving as a base for the ensuing aria, in which melody, harmony, and rhythm inevitably take precedence over the words.

Duprez could thank the high C and the *voix sombrée* for the unique position he enjoyed as the interpreter of certain heavy roles; but the one probably shortened the life of his voice and the other deprived him of that variety of nuance and vocal color that had so distinguished Nourrit's singing of the same repertoire. Duprez may have been driven in his direction by an unconscious desire to compensate for his diminutive size. "What!" screamed a ballet girl when he appeared for the dress rehearsal of his first *William Tell* in Paris. "That toad? Impossible!"

But the intensity of his singing was compelling, and he learned, as so many singers have done, to make up for a voice no longer tractable by various devices of declamation, vocalization, and action, some of them, doubtless, distasteful to a Berlioz. Even such resources are terminable. In 1849 Meyerbeer chose Gustave Roger (1815–1879) instead of Duprez for the role of John of Leyden in *Le prophète*, and Duprez's reign was at an end. He was only forty-three, but he himself conceded that the freshness, brilliance, and flexibility of his voice had diminished, and that, of the resources of his youth, only his strength remained.

Despite Berlioz's captious observations, Duprez seems to have had a compulsive integrity—although possibly not of a kind perceptible to a composer whose precious notation was being ignored. Chorley heard him do *Messiah* (in English) in 1845, and recalled how "this great French tenor, in the strength of his feeling for dramatic truth, propriety and (most of all) his determination never to present himself without doing the best of his best, could sing when his voice was half gone."

Roger heard an *Otello* in 1849 and noted in his diary:

Duprez, today, electrified us all. What daring! A terrifying old lion! How he hurled his guts in the audience's face! For those are no longer notes that one hears. They are the explosion of a breast crushed by an elephant's foot! That's his own blood, his own life, that he is squandering to entice from the public those cries of "Bravo!" with which the Romans honored the dying gladiator. There is a certain nobility about it. For despite the inequalities of a voice more blemished by passion than time, his good schooling prevails, and he finds even in his deficiencies the means of sustaining style. When this man is gone the world will not hear his like again. I was amused by the critics and minor musicians talking about him in the foyer. Some find that he drags, that he opens his mouth too wide, and God knows what else. And what does it all mean? It's molten ore that he pours into those broadened rhythms, and when he opens his mouth so wide it is to show us his heart!

Duprez lived to be eighty-nine, remaining active as a successful teacher and unsuccessful composer. One of his pupils was Marie Miolan-Carvalho (1827–1895), Gounod's first Marguerite and first Juliet. Among the diversions of his declining years was a little marionette theater set up in a corner of his living room where opera scenes were staged, the figures manipulated and their music sung by his son and daughter. Originally intended only for the amusement of family and friends, it achieved such celebrity that a special performance was commanded by Napoleon III. Shades of Guadagni, singing Orpheus behind the scenes of his puppet theater at Padua!

NOTES

Preface (pp. vii–xi)

1. It will be helpful to those who *hear* mentally as they read to know that the French, when pronouncing the names of both Nourrit and Duprez, sound the final consonant.
2. Quicherat, volume three, p. 82. Quicherat's biography, *Adolphe Nourrit: Sa Vie, Son Talent, Son Caractère, Sa Correspondance*, was published by the Librairie de L. Hachette, Paris, 1867. Annotation hereafter refers to volume three unless otherwise indicated.
3. Henry Pleasants, *The Great Singers: From the Dawn of Opera to Our Own Time*, Simon & Schuster, New York, 1966.
4. *The Music Criticisms of Hugo Wolf*, translated and edited by Henry Pleasants, Holmes & Meier, New York, 1978.
5. Friedrich Wieck, *Piano and Song*, translated and edited by Henry Pleasants, Pendragon Press, Stuyvesant, N.Y., 1988.

Introduction (pp. 1–8)

1. Heinz Becker and Gudrun Becker, eds., *Giacomo Meyerbeer: Briefwechsel und Tagebücher*, volume three, Verlag Walter de Cruyter, Berlin, 1975, p. 21.
2. Quicherat, volume two, pp. 399–400.
3. Quicherat, volume one, p. 20.
4. François-Joseph Talma (1763–1826).
5. Quicherat, volume one, p. 13.

Part 1 (pp. 9–27)

1. Alexandre-Étienne Choron (1771–1834), a many-sided French composer, theoretician, pedagogue, and publisher.
2. Charles Édouard Duponchel (1795–1868), an architect and painter, who took over the direction of the Opéra from Louis Véron in 1835, having served there for some years as "chef du service de la scène." He continued as director until 1841.
3. Louis Désiré Véron (1798–1867), founder of the *Revue de Paris* (1829) and director of the Opéra (1831–1836).
4. Letter to Auguste Féréol dated 19 October 1836, Quicherat, pp. 17–24.
5. Letter to Adèle Nourrit, 15 June 1837, in Quicherat, pp. 48–49.
6. Letter from M. G. Bénédit to M. le Directeur de la *Revue Musicale*, published in the issue of 25 April 1839, in Quicherat, pp. 432–433.
7. Ibid., p. 432.
8. Quicherat, volume one, p. 318.
9. Ibid., p. 326.

10. Ibid., p. 330.
11. Letter to Auguste Féréol, 22 November 1837, in Quicherat, pp. 58–62.

Part 2 (pp. 29–42)

1. Letter to Adèle Nourrit from Genoa, 2 January 1838, in Quicherat, pp. 73–74.
2. Letter to Adèle Nourrit, 3 January 1838, in Quicherat, p. 79.
3. Letter to Adèle Nourrit from Milan, 10 January 1838, in Quicherat, pp. 82–83.
4. Ferdinand Hiller (1811–1885), German pianist, composer, conductor, and pedagogue.
5. Johann Peter Pixis (1788–1874), German pianist and pedagogue.
6. Giuditta Pasta (1797–1865), the foremost dramatic soprano of her generation, and Bellini's first Norma. She was nearing the end of a glorious career, and enjoying semi-retirement in a villa on nearby Lake Como. Nourrit had known her in Paris when she was singing at the Théâtre-Italien.
7. Letter to Adèle Nourrit, 10 January 1838, in Quicherat, p. 84.
8. Rossini and his mistress, Olympe Pélissier, had moved from Bologna to Milan in early November 1837, taking rooms in the Palazzo Cantu at the Ponte Damiano. Herbert Weinstock, in his *Rossini* (Alfred A. Knopf, New York, 1968), pp. 199–200, quotes from a letter from Rossini to his friend Carlo Severini: "I am here in Milan enjoying a rather brilliant life. I give musicales or musi-

cal evenings at my home each Friday. I have a handsome apartment, and everyone wants to attend these reunions."

9. Letter to Adèle Nourrit, 12 January 1838, in Quicherat, pp. 88–89.

10. Ibid., pp. 91–93.

11. Letter to Adèle Nourrit, 13 January 1838, in Quicherat, pp. 94–95.

12. Letter to Adèle Nourrit from Venice, 22 January 1838, in Quicherat, p. 29.

13. Properly Karoline Unger (1803–1877), a Viennese contralto now best remembered for having sung with Henriette Sontag in the first performance of Beethoven's Ninth Symphony in 1824. It was she, so the story has come down to us, who had the idea of turning Beethoven around after the conclusion of the symphony so that he could *see* the applause that he could not hear. She sang extensively and successfully in Italy for many years, introducing an *h* after the *g* in her name in order to be assured of a correct pronunciation.

14. Giorgio Ronconi (1810–1890), an outstanding Italian baritone then at the beginning of an illustrious career. He was destined to be Verdi's first Nabucco and the first London Rigoletto.

15. Letter to Adèle Nourrit, 23 January 1838, in Quicherat, pp. 100–102.

16. Napoleone Moriani (1808–1878), destined to provide a footnote to opera history as the presumed father of the two illegitimate children of Verdi's future mistress and wife, Giuseppina Strepponi.

17. A puzzling statement, coming from Nourrit. The note

is an F-natural. But then the opera was not in his repertoire.

18. Letter to Adèle Nourrit, 25 January 1838, in Quicherat, pp. 104–105.
19. Giovanni-Battista Velluti (1781–1861). The last of his kind, the castrato Velluti had a long and distinguished career in Italy and elsewhere, crowned by his singing of the role of Armando in Meyerbeer's *Il crociato in Egitto*, in both Paris and London.
20. Letter to Adèle Nourrit, 30 January 1838, in Quicherat, p. 111.
21. Letter to Adèle Nourrit from Florence, 6 February 1838, in Quicherat, pp. 116–117.
22. Letter to Adèle Nourrit from Rome, 1 March 1838, in Quicherat, pp. 149–152.

Part 3 (pp. 43–81)

1. Domenico Barbaja (1778–1841), the most important opera impresario of his time. He managed the San Carlo and Nuovo theaters in Naples (1809–24), the Kärntnertor Theater and Theater an der Wien in Vienna (1821–28), La Scala and Canobbiana theaters in Milan (1826–32). He produced many works of Bellini, Donizetti, and Rossini, introduced their operas to Vienna, and launched their international circulation.
2. Letter to Adèle Nourrit from Naples, 6 March 1838, in Quicherat, pp. 154–159.
3. Ibid., pp. 158–159.
4. Letter to Adèle Nourrit, 10 March 1838, in Quicherat, pp. 159–160.

5. Letter to Adèle Nourrit, 17 March 1838, in Quicherat, pp. 168–170.

6. Letter to Adèle Nourrit, 20 March 1838, in Quicherat, pp. 173–174.

7. Girolamo Crescentini (1762–1846), a castrato contralto or mezzo-soprano, one of the last and one of the greatest. He was invited by Napoleon to become singing teacher to his family. He lived in Paris from 1806 to 1812, before settling in Naples.

8. Letter to Adèle Nourrit, 20 March 1838, in Quicherat, p. 177.

9. Letter to Adèle Nourrit, 24 March 1838, in Quicherat, pp. 178–179.

10. Ibid., pp. 179–181.

11. Letter to Adèle Nourrit, 30 March 1838, in Quicherat, p. 189.

12. Poleuctas was a second-century Christian martyr, a Roman military officer in Armenia, who became a Christian because of the example of a martyred friend. He refused the demands of the Roman authorities to worship their idols, and destroyed several temples of their deities. He was put to the sword, probably on 7 January A.D. 200. His memory is greatly venerated in the Greek Orthodox Church, which celebrates his feast on 7 January.

13. Letter to Adèle Nourrit, 30 March 1838, in Quicherat, p. 191.

14. Letter to Adèle Nourrit, 4 April 1838, in Quicherat, pp. 191–194.

15. Letter to Adèle Nourrit, 5 April 1838, in Quicherat, pp. 196–198.

16. Giulio Bordogni (1789–1856), Italian tenor and singing

teacher, one of Rossini's tenors. He was a member of the company of the Théâtre-Italien for fourteen years and was appointed to a professorship at the Conservatoire in 1820. He published a "Method" and a number of exercises.

17. Letter to Adèle Nourrit, 10 April 1838, in Quicherat, pp. 215–217.

18. Letter to Adèle Nourrit, 12 April 1838, in Quicherat, p. 224.

19. Letter to Adèle Nourrit, 17 April 1838, in Quicherat, pp. 228–229.

20. Letter to Adèle Nourrit, 29 April 1838, in Quicherat, pp. 246–248.

21. Letter to Adèle Nourrit, 6 May 1838, in Quicherat, p. 257.

22. Letter to Adèle Nourrit, 8 May 1838, in Quicherat, pp. 259–260.

23. Letter from Adèle Nourrit to her brother, Eugène Duverger, in Paris, 26 June 1838, in Quicherat, pp. 405–406.

24. Letter from Adèle Nourrit to Eugène Duverger, 29 June 1838, in Quicherat, pp. 406–407.

25. Letter to Ferdinand Hiller, 6 July 1838, in Quicherat, p. 274.

26. Letter to Eugène Duverger, 26 July 1838, in Quicherat, pp. 276–277.

27. Letter to Eugène Duverger, 16 August 1838, in Quicherat, pp. 280–281.

28. Letter to Madame Aucoc, 4 September 1838, in Quicherat, pp. 282–283.

29. Saverio Mercadante (1795–1870). *Il giuramento*, the most successful of his many operas, had had its premiere

in Milan on 10 March 1838. Mercadante was born in Bari, but grew up in Naples and was accepted as one of them by Neapolitans.

30. Letter to Eugène Duverger, 13 October 1838, in Quicherat, pp. 288–293.

31. Letter to Eugène Duverger, 15 October 1838, in Quicherat, pp. 294–295.

32. Postscript to the letter above, dated 16 October 1838, in Quicherat, p. 295.

33. Letter from Adèle Nourrit to Eugène Duverger, 20 October 1838, in Quicherat, p. 408.

Part 4 (pp. 83–124)

1. Adelina Spech (1811–1866), a contralto or mezzo-soprano, married to the tenor Lorenzo Salvi, who was also in the *Il giuramento* cast.

2. Letter to Eugène Duverger, 25 October 1838, in Quicherat, pp. 297–299.

3. Édouard Bertin (1797–1871), who, with his younger brother, Armand (1801–1854), directed the influential *Journal des Débats* after the death of their father, Louis-François Bertin (1766–1841), its founder. Édouard was also a landscape painter.

4. Letter to Madame Nourrit (his mother), undated but probably 9 November 1838, in Quicherat, pp. 300–301.

5. Letter to Eugène Duverger, 9 November 1838 (it went by the same post as the above), in Quicherat, pp. 302–303.

6. Giuseppe Festa had been the principal conductor at the San Carlo since 1793.

7. Letter to Eugène Duverger, 22 November 1838, in Quicherat, pp. 307–312.

8. Donizetti's *Roberto Devereux*, first performed at the San Carlo on 28 October 1837.

9. Letter to Alexandre Duverger, his father-in-law, 23 November 1838, in Quicherat, pp. 313–314.

10. Gustave Euzet, whose dates I have been unable to determine, remained in France. He had a modest career in provincial houses and, beginning in 1847, at the Opéra.

11. Henri-Bernard Dabadie (1797–1853), a principal baritone at the Opéra and Nourrit's colleague in many important casts including that of *William Tell*, in which Dabadie sang the title role.

12. Letter to Gustave Euzet, January 1839, in Quicherat, pp. 320–322.

13. Letter to Madame Aucoc, 23 January 1839, in Quicherat, pp. 328–330.

14. Giuseppina Ronzi de Begnis (1800–1853), one of the most celebrated sopranos of her time, specializing in the operas of Rossini, Donizetti, Bellini, and Mozart. Her maiden name was Ronzi. She had married, in 1816, the bass Giuseppe de Begnis, from whom she was later divorced.

15. Paul-Bernard (Paolo) Barroilhet (1805–1871), an excellent French baritone who had been for some years a valued member of the San Carlo company.

16. Letter to Louis Quicherat, 5 February 1839, in Quicherat, pp. 334–338.

17. Letter from Adèle Nourrit to Eugène Duverger, 6 February 1839, in Quicherat, pp. 408–410.

18. Letter to Alexandre Duverger, 7 February 1839, in Quicherat, pp. 338–340.

19. Letter to Monsieur A. D., 14 February 1839, in Quicherat, pp. 342–345.

20. Quicherat, in a footnote (p. 348), identifies Loulans as a village in the Haute-Saône, but does not identify the lady beyond describing her as an excellent musician and accompanist, "a veritable phenomenon, who is able to accompany from a full score at sight."

21. Letter to Madame Nourrit (his mother), 23 February 1839, in Quicherat, pp. 347–350.

22. Letter to Alexandre Duverger, 28 February 1839, in Quicherat, pp. 350–351.

23. Ibid., pp. 353–354.

24. Ibid., p. 355.

25. Letter to Luigi Cherubini, 1 March 1839, in Quicherat, pp. 355–358.

26. Letter to Madame Nourrit (his mother), 4 March 1839, in Quicherat, p. 357.

27. Prospero Selli was an obscure Neapolitan opera composer.

28. Granchi had sung Sara, Duchess of Nottingham, in the premiere of Donizetti's *Roberto Devereux* at the San Carlo in 1837.

29. Guillaume (Guglielmo) Cottrau was the director of the Neapolitan publishing house of B. Girard and, obviously, a French intimate of the Nourrit family circle in Naples.

30. Letter of 12 March 1839 from Manuel García, Jr., presumably to Louis Quicherat, as no other addressee is given in Quicherat, pp. 410–413.

31. Nourrit himself had referred to his loss of weight in a letter to an unidentified friend (Monsieur A. D., again) of

10 August 1838, but with no suggestion that it had anything to do with ill health:

> Here I am, a debutant, beginning a new career, and by a singular coincidence, I begin it in the same month in which I made my debut in France! Let that be a favorable augury. You know that I arrived in Naples on my birthday. Again a singular coincidence. It is, in effect, a new life into which I am reborn. Everything about my physical appearance has had to change. From the fat fellow I used to be I have become almost skinny. I used to have an almost feminine physiognomy (when I was young); now my face is covered by a black beard. (Quicherat, p. 278)

Also, as quoted earlier, in a letter to his father-in-law of 23 November 1838, Nourrit had commented: "Compatriots who hear me compliment me on my progress and loss of weight." (Quicherat, p. 314)

32. Letter from Barroilhet addressed to M. Duverger (whether father or son is not specified in Quicherat, but it was probably the latter), undated, but Quicherat accepts that it is of March 1839. In Quicherat, pp. 413–414.

33. Paul Desmarie, *Moeurs italiennes* (1860), in Quicherat, pp. 416–418.

34. Curtis Cate, *George Sand: A Biography*, Hamish Hamilton, London, 1975, p. 480.

Epilogue (pp. 125–131)

1. Letter to Auguste Féréol, 22 November 1837, in Quicherat, p. 58.

2. Letter to Quicherat from Manuel García, Jr., 12 March 1839, in Quicherat, pp. 410–411.

3. Letter to Duverger from Barroilhet, March 1839, in Quicherat, p. 413.

Postscripts (pp. 133–162)

1. Henry Fothergill Chorley, *Music and Manners in France and Germany (1841–44)*, Longman, Brown, Green and Longmans, London, 1844, volume one, pp. 61–76.

2. Leopoldo Tarantini in *Salvator Rosa: Album artistico, scientifico e litterario*, 18 November 1838, in Quicherat, volume two, pp. 521–523. Tarantini was a Neapolitan critic and poet, a number of whose poems were set to music by Donizetti.

3. Bellini's earlier stagework, *Adelson e Salvini,* had been given at the Naples Conservatory of S. Sebastiano the previous year. The name Gernando replaced Fernando because the Neapolitan censors forbade the use of the name of a ruler of the Kingdom of the Two Sicilies. When Bellini revised this work for Genoa in 1828, the original title, *Bianca e Fernando,* was restored.

4. Herbert Weinstock, *Vincenzo Bellini,* Alfred A. Knopf, New York, 1971, pp. 39–40.

5. Pleasants, *The Great Singers,* p. 133.

6. Henry Chorley, *Thirty Years' Musical Recollections*, 1862; reprint, Alfred A. Knopf, New York, 1926, p. 21.

7. Quicherat, p. 82.

8. Chorley, *Thirty Years' Musical Recollections,* p. 23.

INDEX

Auber, Daniel-François-Esprit, 2
  Gustave III, vii, 152, plate 11
  La muette de Portici, vii, 14,
    19, 22, 23, 24, 69, 152,
    plate 6
  Le philtre, 23
Aucoc, Madame (sister of
    Nourrit), 71, 98, 169, 171

Barbaja, Domenico, 47, 50, 54,
    56, 57, 61, 63–64, 65, 67,
    75–76, 79, 87, 94, 100,
    108, 112, 118, 122
Barbò, Giacomo di Castelmorano,
    147
Barroilhet, Paul-Bernard (Paolo),
    102, 118–119, 129
Bassadonna, Giovanni, 57, 76
Beer, Jakob. *See* Meyerbeer,
    Giacomo
Begnis, Giuseppe de, 171
Bellini, Vincenzo, 2, 147
  Adelson e Salvini, 174
  Bianca e Fernando, 147, 174
  Norma, 3, 95, 100, 102, 105,
    107, 111, 117, 131, 150

Il pirata, 147
I Puritani, 38, 147
  La sonnambula, 102, 147
Bénédit, M. G., 20, 22
Bergonzi, Carlo, 1
Berlioz, Hector, 141, 156–158
Bertin, Armand, 170
Bertin, Édouard, 87, 89, 170
Bertin, Louis-François, 170
Bizet, Georges, 4
Bjoerling, Jussi, 1
Boieldieu, François-Adrien, 19
  La dame blanche, 19
Boisselot, Xavier, 21, 22
Bordogni, Giulio, 61

Cammarano, Salvatore, 53
Campanini, Italo, 152
Carreras, José, 1, 146
Caruso, Enrico, 1, 146, 152
Cate, Curtis, 123, 173
Cherubini, Luigi, 114, 124
Chopin, Frédéric, 123–124, 156
Chorley, Henry Fothergill, 139,
    148, 151, 161, 174
Choron, Alexandre-Étienne, 11

175

Corelli, Franco, 1
Cottrau, Guillaume (Guglielmo), 118, 120, 172
Crescentini, Girolamo, 50–51, 93, 168

Dabadie, Henri-Bernard, 98, 171
David, Giacomo, 146
David, Giovanni, 2, 146, 147, 154
Delacroix, Eugène, 76
Dérancourt, Desiderata, 33
Desmaire, Paul, 120, 173
Deveria, Jacques Jean, plate 2
Di Stefano, Giuseppe, 1
Domingo, Placido, 1, 146, 149, 150
Donizetti, Gaetano, v, viii, 37, 40, 43, 45–53, 55, 56, 57, 60, 63, 77, 86, 97, 106–107, 130
  Lucia di Lammermoor, 33, 50, 63, 148, 150, 158
  Maria de Rudenz, 36
  Les martyrs, 54
  Pia de' Tolomei, 72, 74, 75, 76, 79, 86, 87, 89–90, 94
  Poliuto (Polyeucte), v, viii, 43, 53, 66, 70, 73–74, 81, 93, 106–107, 130, 168
  Roberto Devereux, 94, 171
Donzelli, Domenico, 2, 4, 6, 55, 56, 150, 154, 155
Duponchel, Charles Édouard, 12, 13, 15, 17, 92
Duprez, Gilbert-Louis, viii, 3, 4, 11, 12, 13, 16, 18, 24, 25, 26, 52, 54, 105, 124, 140, 142, 143, 150, 152–153, 155, 156–161, plate 3
Duverger, Alexandre (Nourrit's father-in-law), 8, 95
Duverger, Eugène (Nourrit's brother-in-law), 19, 70, 72, 78, 88, 119, 123, 129, 173

Euzet, Gustave, 96–98

Ferdinand II, king, 71, 73,
Féréol, Auguste, 11, 19, 23, 127
Festa, Giuseppe, 90, 170
Forcade, Dr., 22

Garcìa, Madame Manuel, 49
Garcìa, Manuel, 2, 5, 6, 7, 8, 146, 147, 150, 153, 154, plate 4
Garcìa, Manuel, Jr., 6, 71, 114, 117, 118, 128–129, plate 5
Garrick, David, 145
Gaveaux, Pierre, 19
Gedda, Nicolai, 1
Gigli, Beniamino, 1
Giordano, Umberto, 4
Gluck, Christoph Willibald, 5, 7, 18, plate 10
Gounod, Charles François, 4, 162
Granci, Almeridna, 117, 172
Guadagni, Gaetano, 162

Halévy, Jacques-François-Fromental-Élie, 2, 17, 154
  Guido et Ginevra, 16

La Juive, vii, viii, 15, 16, 19, 20–21, 23, 24, 143, 152, 154, plate 8

Handel, George Frideric, 161

Hérold, Louis-Joseph-Ferdinand, 108, 112

Hiller, Ferdinand, 33, 34, 36, 40, 70

Inchindi, Giovanni, 31

Latka, Count P., 41

Lauri-Volpi, Giacomo, 1

Legouvé, Ernest, 148

Leitner, Karl, 123

Leoncavallo, Ruggiero, 4

Lillo, Giuseppe, 38

Liszt, Franz (Ferenc), ix, 33, 34, 35, 156

Lorenz, Max, 1

Louis, M. (physician), 24

Malibran, Maria, 6, 36

Mario (tenor), 146

Martinelli, Giovanni, 1, 152

Mascagni, Pietro, 4

Massenet, Jules, 4

Melchior, Lauritz, 1

Menelli, Bartolomeo, 41, 54–55

Mercadante, Saverio, viii, 55, 77, 92, 93, 95, 101, 102, 108, 111, 118, 131
  Elena da Feltre, 93, 95, 100
  Gabriella di Vergy, 111, 112, 113, 114
  Il giuramento, viii, 77, 79, 85, 87, 88, 89, 94, 95, 100, 101, 102, 104, 105, 118, 131, 143, 144, 145

Meyerbeer, Giacomo, 3, 6, 154
  L'Africaine, 3
  Il crociato in Egitto, 6, 167
  Les Huguenots, vii, 3, 6, 18, 23, 24, 79, 152
  Le prophète, 3, 161
  Robert le diable, vii, 6, 15, 23, 104, 108, 109, 139, 143, 152, plate 9

Miolan-Carvalho, Marie, 162

Moriani, Napoleone, 38

Mozart, Wolfgang Amadeus, 93, plate 12

Napoleon III, emperor, 162

Nicholas I, czar, 151

Nourrit, Adèle (wife), x, 8, 18, 19, 23, 49, 67–68, 69–70, 73, 74, 80, 85, 88, 105, 110, 112–113, 118, 123, 124

Nourrit, Adolphe, roles he sang (composer, opera, role)
  Auber, *Gustave III*, Gustave, vii, 152, plate 11
    La muette de Portici, Masaniello, vii, 14, 19, 22, 23, 69, 152, plate 6
    Le philtre, Guillaume, 23
  Bellini, *Norma*, Pollione, 95, 100, 102–103, 105, 111, 117, 131
  Boieldieu, *La dame blanche*, Georges Brown, 19
  Gaveaux, *Le bouffe et le tailleur*, Cavalieri, 19

[Nourrit, Adolphe]
Gluck, *Armide*, Renaud, 5, 7,
    18
  Orfeo ed Euridice, Orphée,
    5, plate 10
  Iphigénie en Tauride,
    Pylades, 5, 18
Halévy, *La Juive*, Éléazar, vii,
    viii, 4, 15, 16, 19,
    20–21, 23, 69, 143,
    152, 154, plate 8
Mercadante, *Elena da Feltre*,
    Reina, 93, 95, 101
  Il giuramento, Viscardo,
    viii, 77, 79, 85, 87–89,
    94, 95, 100–102, 104,
    105, 118, 131, 143,
    144, 145, 170
Meyerbeer, *Les Huguenots*,
    Raoul, vii–viii, 3, 4, 6,
    18, 23, 69, 152, plate 9
  Robert le diable, Robert,
    vii, 4, 15, 19, 23, 69,
    104, 108, 109, 139,
    143, 152, plate 7
Mozart, *Don Giovanni*, Don
    Juan, 93, plate 12
Rossini, *Le Comte Ory*, Count
    Ory, vii, 19, 152
  Moïse, Aménophis, vii, 152
  Otello, Otello, 154
  Le siège de Corinthe,
    Néoclès, vii, 6, 152,
    153
  William Tell, Arnold, vii,
    4, 13, 19, 22, 23, 33,
    50, 55–57, 62, 76, 77,
    143, 152

Spontini, *Fernand Cortez*,
    Cortez, 23
Nourrit, Madame (mother), 18,
    87, 114, 170, 172
Nozzari, Andrea, 2, 146, 147, 154
Ober, William B., Dr., 135–136

Pacini, Giovanni, plate 14
Paër, Ferdinando, 5, 6
Pasta, Giuditta, 33, 39
Pavarotti, Luciano, 1, 146, 149,
    150
Peerce, Jan, 154
Pélissier, Olympe, 165
Perrucchini, Signor, 39
Persiani, Fanny Tacchinardi, 39
Persiani, Giuseppe, 102
Pertile, Aureliano, 1
Piccinni, Niccolò, 5
Pisaroni, Benedetta Rosamunda,
    39, 158
Pixis, Francilla, 33, 111
Pixis, Johann Peter, 33
Pleasants, Richard, ix, x

Quicherat, Louis, ix, 3, 4, 5, 8,
    101, 107, 120, 143, 149

Reszke, Jean de, 146, 152
Rocca, Francesco, Dr., 119, 129
Roger, Gustave, 161
Ronconi, Giorgio, 36, 37, 38–39
Ronzi de Begnis, Giuseppina,
    102, 171
Rossini, Gioachino, 2, 5, 6,
    32–36, 41, 42, 45, 50, 54,
    55, 94, 147, 151
  Il barbiere di Siviglia, 5

Le Comte Ory, vii, 19, 32, 55, 152

Elisabetta, regina d'Inghilterra, 147

Maometto II, 6, 147

Moïse, vii, 32, 152

Otello, 3, 93, 94, 147, 154, 161

Le siège de Corinthe, vii, 6, 32, 147, 152, 153

William Tell, vii, 13, 22, 23, 24, 32, 33, 35, 50, 55–57, 61, 62, 76, 77, 79, 85, 93, 112, 143, 152, 153, 157, 158–160

Roswaenge, Helge, 1

Rubini, Adelaide Comelli (wife), 151

Rubini, Giovanni-Battista, 2, 3, 26, 32, 38, 104, 105, 110, 143, 146–151, 154, plate 2

Salvi, Lorenzo, 90, 170

Sand, George, 123–124, 156

Sargent, John Singer, plate 5

Schipa, Tito, 1

Schröder-Devrient, Wilhelmine, 153, 154

Schubert, Franz, ix, 39, 59, 63, 123, 154, 156

Schumann, Clara, ix

Scribe, Eugène, 54, 93

Scudo, Pierre, 148

Selli, Prospero, 115, 116, 172

Slezak, Leo, 152

Sontag, Henriette, 166

Spech, Adelina, 85, 102

Spontini, Gasparo, 23

Stephens, Joseph H., Dr., 135, 136–137

Strauss, Richard, 4

Strepponi, Giuseppina, 166

Talma, François-Joseph, 6, 7, 8, 145, 150, 153

Tamagno, Francesco, 152

Tamberlik, Enrico, 152

Tarantini, Leopoldo, 143, 174

Tauber, Richard, 1

Tichatschek, Joseph Aloys, 152

Tucker, Richard, 1, 154

Unger, Karoline, 36, 37, 39

Velluti, Giovanni-Battista, 39

Verdi, Giuseppe, 3, 4, 152

Véron, Louis Désiré, 12

Viardot, Pauline, 6

Vigneron, Pierre Roch, ii

Wagner, Richard, x, 4, 152

Wartel, Pierre François, 15

Weinstock, Herbert, 147, 174

Wieck, Friedrich, ix

Wolf, Hugo, ix

Photograph Credits

Frontispiece and Plate 3   The Music Division, The New York Public Library for the Performing Arts, Astor, Lenox and Tilden Foundations.

Plates 1 and 2   The Royal College of Music, London.

Plates 4, 5, 6, 8, 10, 11, and 12   The Theatre Museum, courtesy of the Trustees of the Victoria and Albert Museum, London.

Plates 7 and 9   Bibliothèque-Musée de l'Opéra, Paris; photographs courtesy of *Opera News*.

Plates 13 and 14   Frances L. Hofer bequest, Harvard Theatre Collection, Harvard College Library, Cambridge, Massachusetts.

Postscripts: The Three Tenors of the 1830s

The biographical sketch of Rubini is slightly adapted from an article that appeared in *The Opera Quarterly*, volume ten, number two (winter 1993–94), pp. 100–104. It is reprinted here with kind permission.

The sketches of Nourrit and Duprez are reprinted from Henry Pleasants, *The Great Singers: From the Dawn of Opera to Our Own Time*, Simon & Schuster, New York, 1966. Copyright Henry Pleasants.